FLYING SCHOOL

The Wright *Flyer* model is for display only. The Lock
rather fragile landing gear and should be flown where
tall grass or low bushes. The Lockheed *Vega* propeller

The models were engineered by Nick Taylor

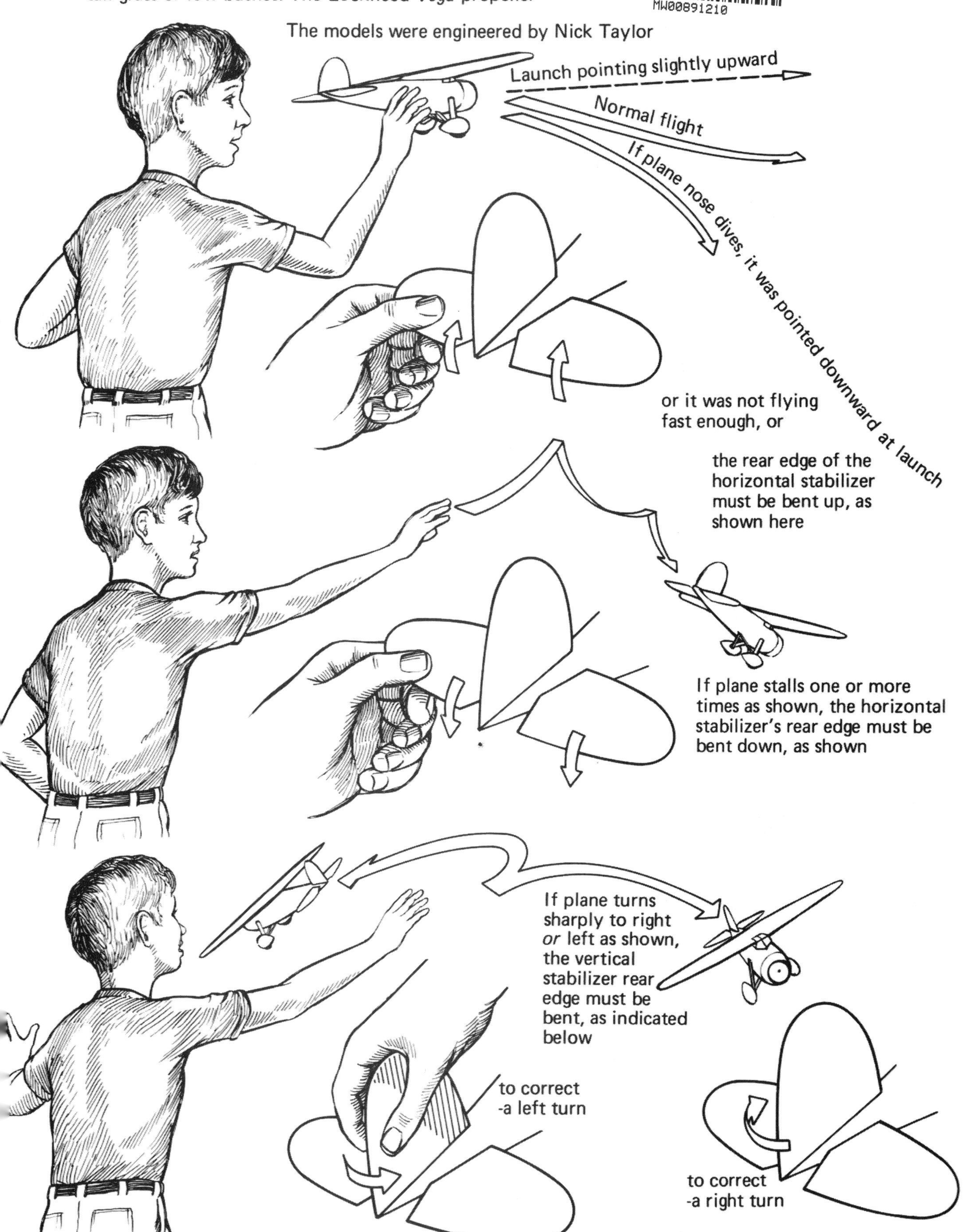

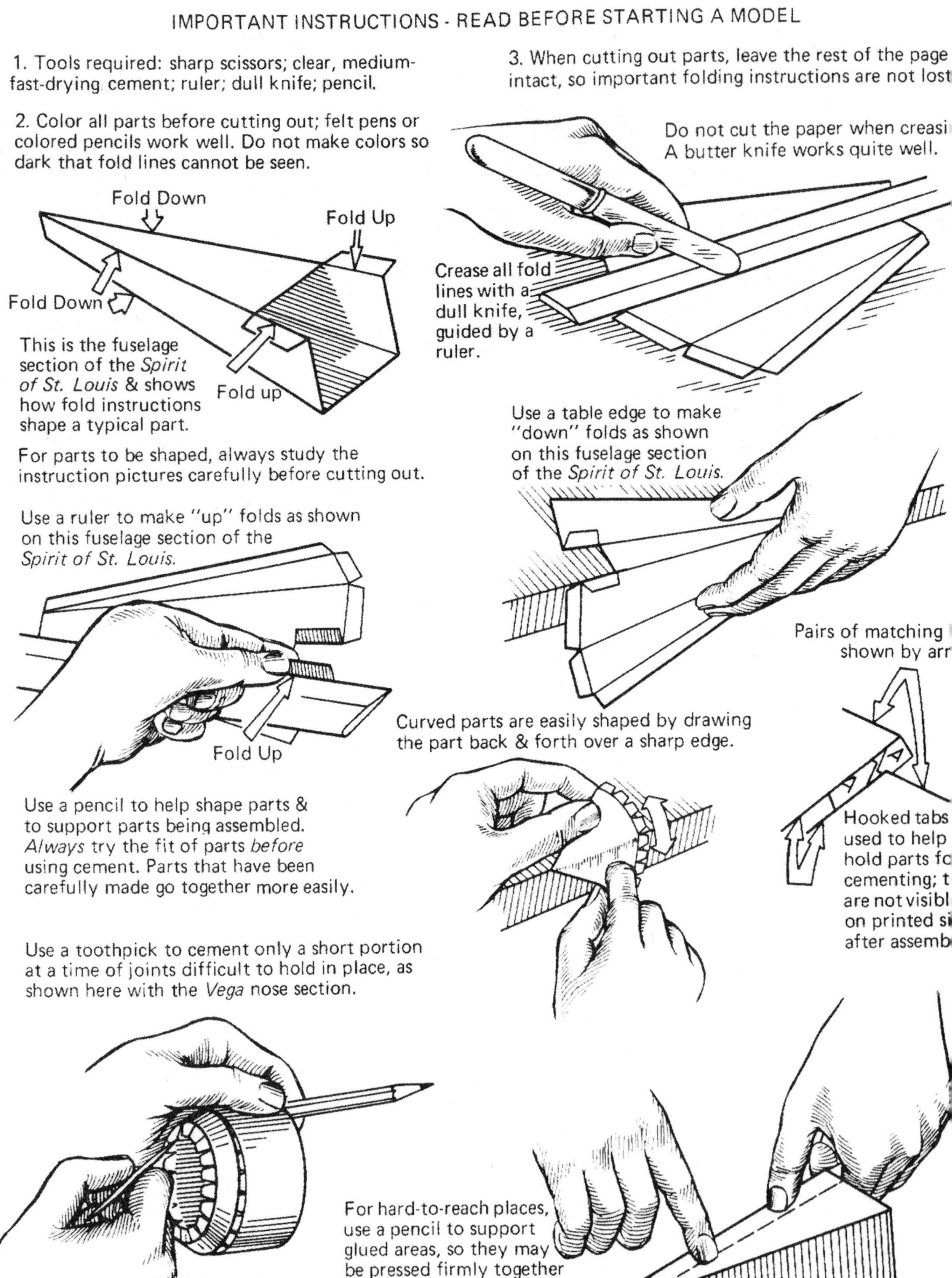
IMPORTANT INSTRUCTIONS - READ BEFORE STARTING A MODEL
1. Tools required: sharp scissors; clear, medium-fast-drying cement; ruler; dull knife; pencil.
2. Color all parts before cutting out; felt pens or colored pencils work well. Do not make colors so dark that fold lines cannot be seen.
Fold Down
Fold Up
Fold Down
This is the fuselage section of the *Spirit of St. Louis* & shows how fold instructions shape a typical part.
Fold up
For parts to be shaped, always study the instruction pictures carefully before cutting out.
Use a ruler to make "up" folds as shown on this fuselage section of the *Spirit of St. Louis.*
Fold Up
Use a pencil to help shape parts & to support parts being assembled. *Always* try the fit of parts *before* using cement. Parts that have been carefully made go together more easily.
Use a toothpick to cement only a short portion at a time of joints difficult to hold in place, as shown here with the *Vega* nose section.
3. When cutting out parts, leave the rest of the page intact, so important folding instructions are not lost
Do not cut the paper when creasi
A butter knife works quite well.
Crease all fold lines with a dull knife, guided by a ruler.
Use a table edge to make "down" folds as shown on this fuselage section of the *Spirit of St. Louis.*
Pairs of matching
shown by arr
Curved parts are easily shaped by drawing the part back & forth over a sharp edge.
Hooked tabs
used to help
hold parts fo
cementing; t
are not visibl
on printed si
after assemb
For hard-to-reach places, use a pencil to support glued areas, so they may be pressed firmly together -as shown for the fuselage section of the *Spirit of St. Louis.*

THE WRIGHT FLYER

On December 17, 1903, near Kittyhawk, North Carolina, the Wright brothers became the first men to fly in a heavier-than-air, engine-powered craft. With Orville at the controls the fragile-looking *Flyer* rose several feet above the ground and remained aloft for twelve seconds. Three more flights were made that day; the last, piloted by Wilbur, covered a distance of 852 feet and lasted 50 seconds. For three years the brothers had come to the open space, ocean winds, and soft sands of Kittyhawk to conduct their experiments with box kites and gliders, all aimed at learning the basics of flying, before building a craft with engine and propellers. It was through this work that they made their most important discovery, namely, that certain controls were absolutely essential for flight. These are: controls that would permit the pilot to point the nose up, down, left, or right, and controls that would permit the pilot to raise or lower a wing tip as desired. These basic controls are to be found on the most modern aircraft and were first used by the Wrights on manned gliders and later on the original *Flyer.*

Orville and Wilbur returned to their Dayton, Ohio, home after telegraphing their father on December 18 with the news of their success and instructions to notify the press. Only three papers bothered to report the event, and one of these didn't even give the story front page space. Recognition would be slow in coming to the brothers partially because the difference between the *Flyer* and balloon flight was not commonly understood. They were after all both "air ships" from the public's point of view. In addition, fanciful newspaper reports of the time only added to the prevailing skepticism. Ironically, it created an ideal climate for the Wrights to continue their work unhampered by reporters and curious onlookers. By 1905 their latest *Flyer* had flown 24.2 miles in 38 minutes 3 seconds on October 5 near Dayton, Ohio. Within two years world governments would be negotiating to purchase their invention and an Aeronautical Division would be set up in the Office of the Chief Signal Officer of the U.S. Army, the ancestor of the U.S. Air Force.

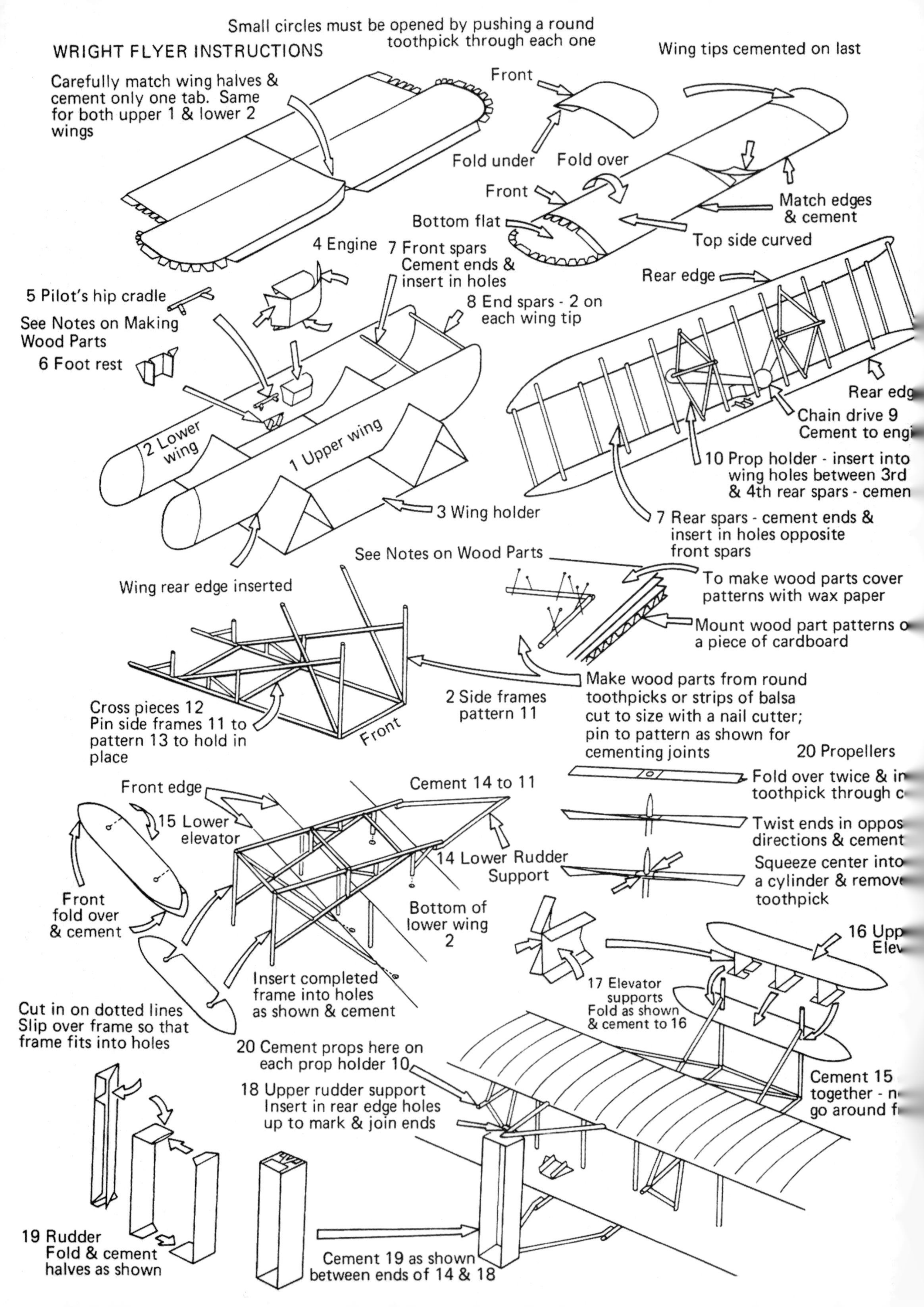
WRIGHT FLYER INSTRUCTIONS
Small circles must be opened by pushing a round toothpick through each one
Wing tips cemented on last
Carefully match wing halves & cement only one tab. Same for both upper 1 & lower 2 wings
Front
Fold under
Fold over
Front
Match edges & cement
Bottom flat
Top side curved
4 Engine
7 Front spars Cement ends & insert in holes
Rear edge
5 Pilot's hip cradle
8 End spars - 2 on each wing tip
See Notes on Making Wood Parts
6 Foot rest
Rear edg
Chain drive 9 Cement to engi
2 Lower wing
1 Upper wing
10 Prop holder - insert into wing holes between 3rd & 4th rear spars - cemen
3 Wing holder
7 Rear spars - cement ends & insert in holes opposite front spars
See Notes on Wood Parts
Wing rear edge inserted
To make wood parts cover patterns with wax paper
Mount wood part patterns o a piece of cardboard
Make wood parts from round toothpicks or strips of balsa cut to size with a nail cutter; pin to pattern as shown for cementing joints
2 Side frames pattern 11
Cross pieces 12 Pin side frames 11 to pattern 13 to hold in place
Front
20 Propellers
Front edge
Cement 14 to 11
Fold over twice & in toothpick through c
15 Lower elevator
Twist ends in oppos directions & cement
14 Lower Rudder Support
Squeeze center into a cylinder & remove toothpick
Front fold over & cement
Bottom of lower wing 2
16 Upp Elev
Insert completed frame into holes as shown & cement
17 Elevator supports Fold as shown & cement to 16
Cut in on dotted lines Slip over frame so that frame fits into holes
20 Cement props here on each prop holder 10
Cement 15 together - n go around f
18 Upper rudder support Insert in rear edge holes up to mark & join ends
19 Rudder Fold & cement halves as shown
Cement 19 as shown between ends of 14 & 18

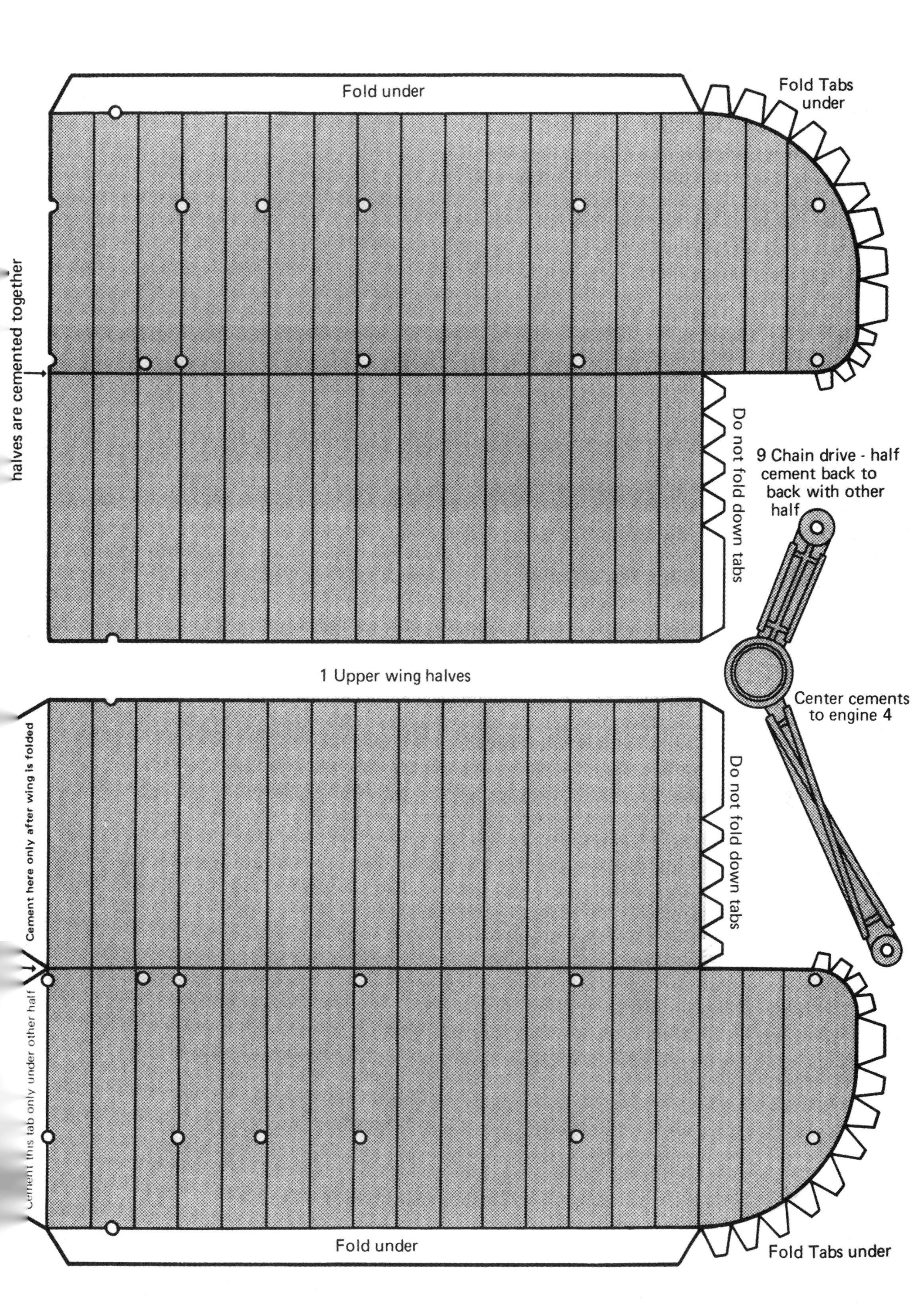
Fold under
Fold Tabs under
halves are cemented together
Do not fold down tabs
9 Chain drive - half cement back to back with other half
1 Upper wing halves
Center cements to engine 4
Cement here only after wing is folded
Do not fold down tabs
Cement this tab only under other half
Fold under
Fold Tabs under

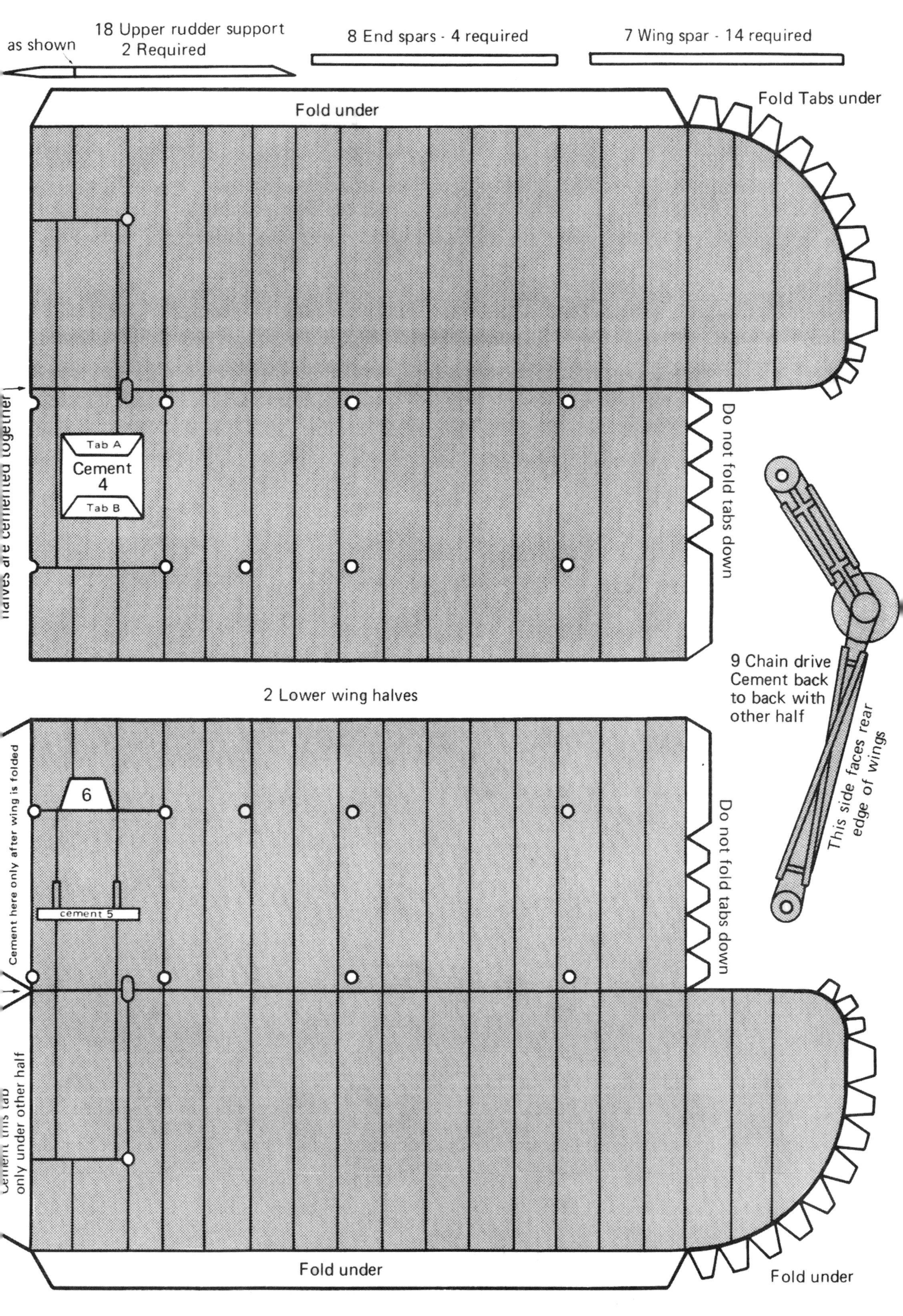
as shown
18 Upper rudder support
2 Required
8 End spars - 4 required
7 Wing spar - 14 required
Fold under
Fold Tabs under
Tab A
Cement
4
Tab B
Do not fold tabs down
halves are cemented together
9 Chain drive
Cement back
to back with
other half
This side faces rear
edge of wings
2 Lower wing halves
6
cement 5
Cement here only after wing is folded
Do not fold tabs down
Cement this tab
only under other half
Fold under
Fold under

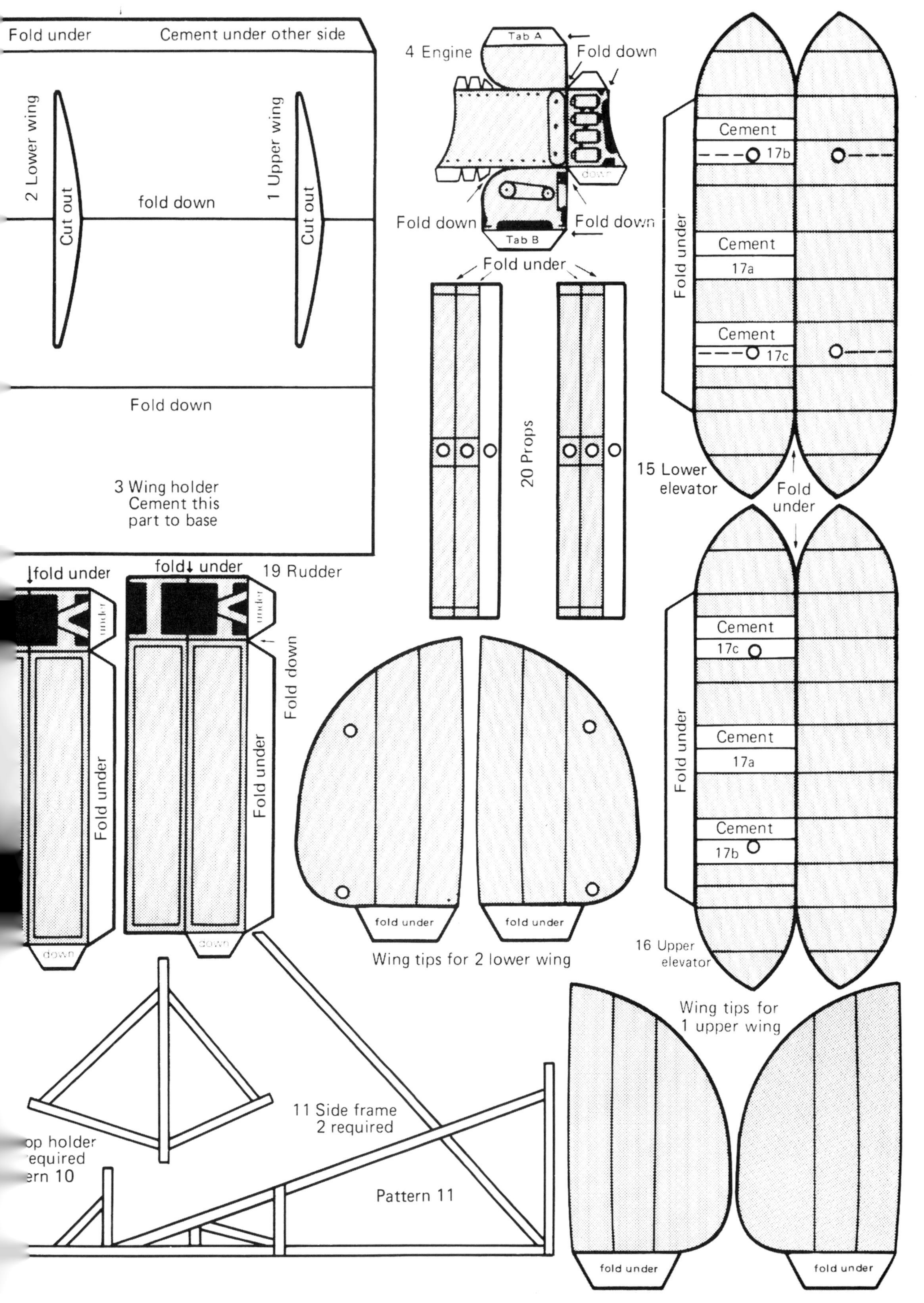
Fold under
Cement under other side
2 Lower wing
Cut out
fold down
1 Upper wing
Cut out
Fold down
3 Wing holder
Cement this part to base
4 Engine
Tab A
Fold down
Fold down
Fold down
Tab B
Fold under
20 Props
Fold under
Cement
17b
Cement
17a
Cement
17c
15 Lower elevator
Fold under
Fold under
Cement
17c
Cement
17a
Cement
17b
16 Upper elevator
fold under
fold under
19 Rudder
under
under
Fold down
Fold under
Fold under
down
down
fold under
fold under
Wing tips for 2 lower wing
Wing tips for 1 upper wing
fold under
fold under
11 Side frame
2 required
Pattern 11
op holder
equired
ern 10

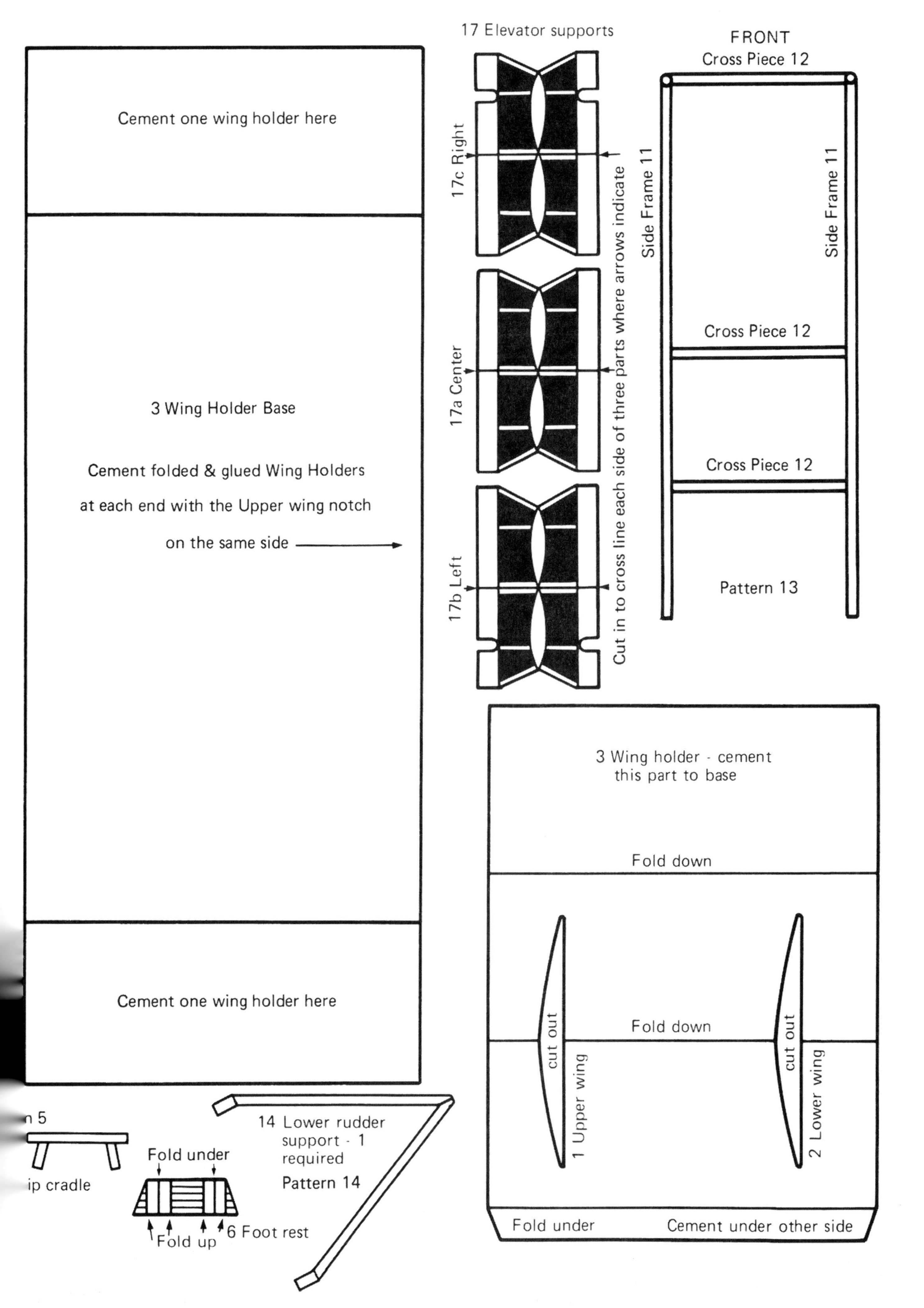
17 Elevator supports
FRONT
Cross Piece 12
Cement one wing holder here
17c Right
Side Frame 11
Side Frame 11
Cut in to cross line each side of three parts where arrows indicate
Cross Piece 12
17a Center
3 Wing Holder Base
Cement folded & glued Wing Holders
at each end with the Upper wing notch
on the same side
Cross Piece 12
17b Left
Pattern 13
3 Wing holder - cement
this part to base
Fold down
Cement one wing holder here
Fold down
cut out
cut out
1 Upper wing
2 Lower wing
n 5
14 Lower rudder
support - 1
required
Pattern 14
Fold under
ip cradle
Fold up
6 Foot rest
Fold under
Cement under other side

On the night of May 21, 1927, twenty-five-year-old Charles Lindbergh landed his Ryan monoplane, *Spirit of St. Louis,* in France to become the first aviator to fly from New York to Paris. He had remained at the controls in his cramped cockpit for 33½ hours and, aided only by the simplest of navigational instruments, had flown more than twice the distance of the first transatlantic flight, made in 1919 by British flyers John Alcock and Arthur Whitten Brown. Most importantly, he had done it alone, in a single-engine plane, and without the backing of a large, well-financed organization.

The dangers involved in the feat were only too well emphasized by the fate of two airmen days before. On May 8, Charles Nungesser, France's third-ranking World War I Ace, and his navigator Francois Coli had posed confidently for photographers in the open cockpit of their biplane, *'L'Oiseau blanc,' (White Bird),* before taking off from Paris for New York. Last sighted over Ireland, they disappeared into the stormy gloom over the Atlantic and were never heard from again. A year earlier René Fonck, the leading Allied war-time ace with 75 victories, had crashed on take-off from Roosevelt Field, New York, in a huge three-engine Sikorsky biplane while attempting a transatlantic crossing. Two of his three crewmen died in the flaming wreckage. The crash pointed out one of the greatest hazards of the Atlantic flight, namely, getting the heavy fuel load off the ground safely to begin with. After that there were possible navigational errors, engine failure, and storms. And, because the shortest route lay well north of the shipping lanes, the pilots faced the certain knowledge that a crash at sea would hold no hope of rescue.

Lindbergh was quite familiar with flying under adverse conditions. Piloting a war-surplus biplane between St. Louis and Chicago, he and a small number of dedicated men flew the U.S. Mail on schedule regardless of the weather. Earlier, he had worked as a barnstormer, flying from one small pasture to the next, hoping to entice the curious to pay a few dollars for a ride over their home town. When the airplane was no longer a novelty, it became increasingly difficult to make expenses with wing walking, stunts, and trick parachute jumps, so he joined the U.S. Army Air Service. No sooner had he received his wings than he found himself discharged from active duty; under the peacetime budget, the service could not afford too many pilots. Signing up to fly the mail, he ended up at Lambert Field in St. Louis, and it was here that his Atlantic odyssey was to begin.

Aircraft design had improved dramatically under the pressures of World War I. Planes of the twenties had reached the point where longer and longer flights were a real possiblilty, and there wasn't any shortage of courageous, eager young pilots ready to assault the barriers of time and distance by air. The Atlantic was a natural objective. To promote its conquest Raymond Orteig, a New York hotel owner, had offered a $25,000 prize to the first plane to fly between New York and Paris. Lindbergh had managed to convince a small number of St. Louis businessmen to back him financially in his attempt at the prize. Meanwhile, others were setting about the same goal, but they were flyers of international reputation capable of raising fortunes to command the best in planes and organizations to plan the venture. By comparison, Lindbergh's chances did not look good. For one thing, his idea of flying alone was generally regarded as suicidal. Furthermore, he was unknown, not a personality who could easily attract donations of fuel, oil, and support from equipment manufacturers. Nonetheless, armed with a winning smile and a boundless confidence in his mission he started to make it all happen. He was promptly turned down in his bid to purchase the Wright-Ballanca, which was regarded as the hottest new plane at that time. The company feared the adverse publicity that would result if the young flyer were sent off in their plane on a foolhardy trip that was sure to end in tragedy. Lindbergh instead turned to another group of young people who like himself were unknown but enthusiastic: the Ryan Aircraft Company in San Diego, California. Together they designed the *Spirit of St. Louis,* which was named by Lindbergh's backers in the hope that the plane's success would promote St. Louis as a center of aviation. Essentially, the *Spirit* was a highly modified Ryan M-2 monoplane. To carry the heavy fuel load in the extra tanks that were installed the wings had to be lengthened ten feet. Lindbergh wanted the pilot's position to be aft of the large fuselage tank because in the event of a crash he didn't want to be crushed between the tank and the engine. This meant there would be no windscreen or forward vision, so a small periscope was built into the instrument panel to give at least a limited look forward. Lindbergh felt there wasn't anything out over the Atlantic to run into anyway; he could land skewed slightly sideways and straighten out just before the wheels touched using one of his two little side windows to see the runway. He stayed with the plane as it took shape, teaching himself navigation when he wasn't active in the actual design of the craft. One of his main concerns was cutting the weight as much as possible; he reasoned that every pound carried required a corresponding amount of fuel that had to be lifted into the air at take-off. He even refused $1,000 to take along a packet of letters for

Charles Lindbergh in the *Spirit of St. Louis*

a stamp collector. Wing struts were covered with balsa wood covers and a hand-beaten aluminum cowling was fitted over the engine, all to reduce the drag. The press had carried daily reports of the expected departure of the other contenders, and as the work neared completion, word was received on Nungesser's take-off from Paris. It seemed that even though they had taken only three months to build the *Spirit,* someone else would be the recipient of the Ortieg prize. In flying the completed plane east to St. Louis he encountered engine trouble and considered turning back, but managed to continue. Later, in New York, some added equipment fixed the engine problem.

As Lindbergh was making his preflight preparations, Nungesser's disappearance added to the tension. The press had swarmed over the flyer from the moment of his arrival in New York and infuriated him with false information not only about his flight but about his personal life as well. A naturally reserved person with a strong sense of personal integrity, Lindbergh was never to have an easy time with most reporters.

On the morning of May 20, the *Spirit of St. Louis* lumbered down the soggy clay runway of Roosevelt Field, cleared the trees at the end of the field by a bare twenty feet, and headed for Paris, France. Lindbergh's life and the future of aviation would never be the same.

Two weeks later the Wright-Ballanca would be flown three hundred miles further into Germany non-stop from New York. The plane that Lindbergh had originally wanted was piloted by Clarence D. Chamberlain.

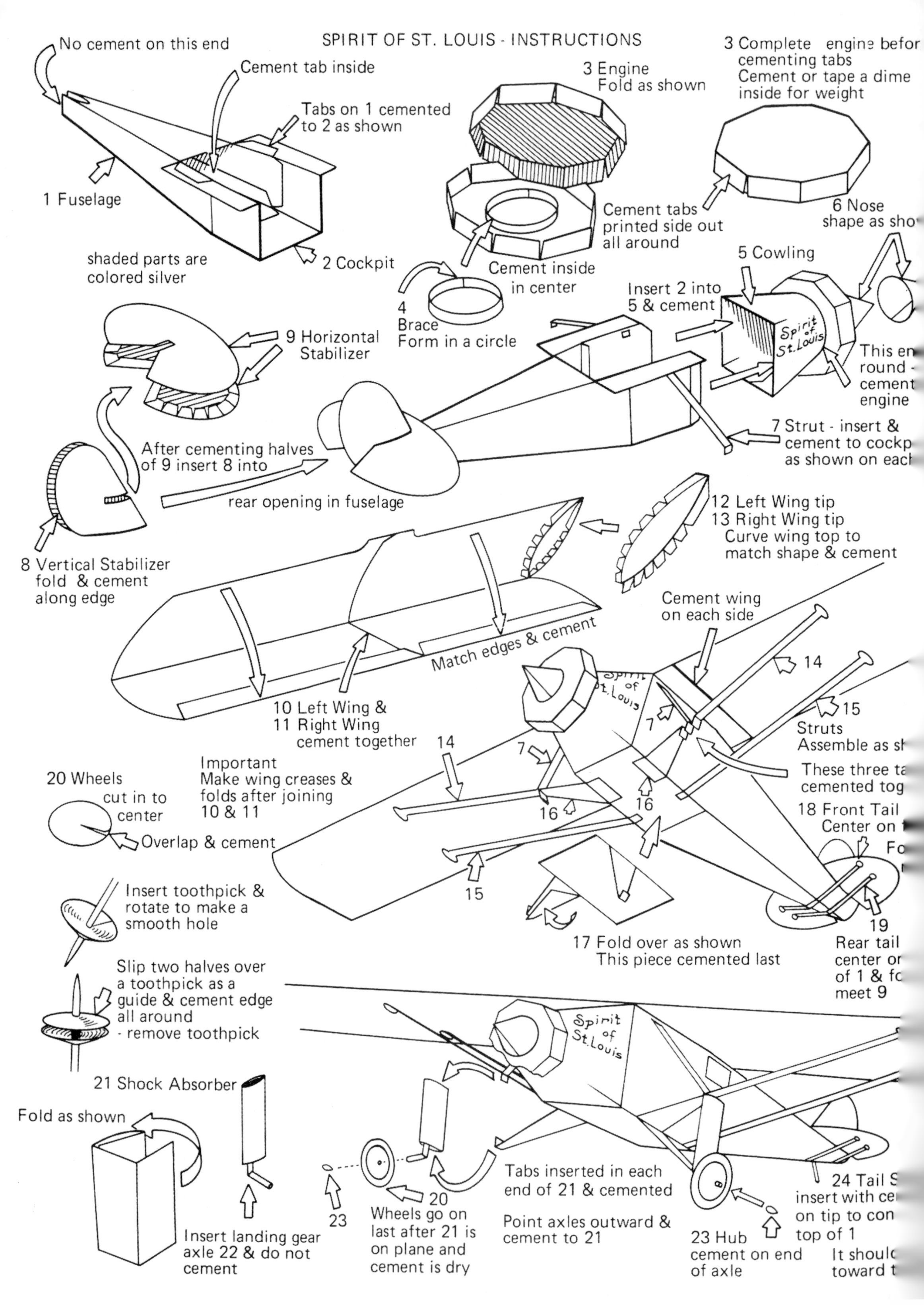

SPIRIT OF ST. LOUIS - INSTRUCTIONS
No cement on this end
Cement tab inside
Tabs on 1 cemented to 2 as shown
1 Fuselage
2 Cockpit
shaded parts are colored silver
3 Engine
Fold as shown
Cement tabs printed side out all around
Cement inside in center
4 Brace
Form in a circle
3 Complete engine befor
cementing tabs
Cement or tape a dime inside for weight
6 Nose
shape as sho
5 Cowling
Insert 2 into 5 & cement
Spirit of St. Louis
This en
round -
cement
engine
7 Strut - insert & cement to cockp
as shown on each
9 Horizontal Stabilizer
After cementing halves of 9 insert 8 into
rear opening in fuselage
8 Vertical Stabilizer
fold & cement along edge
12 Left Wing tip
13 Right Wing tip
Curve wing top to match shape & cement
Match edges & cement
10 Left Wing &
11 Right Wing
cement together
Cement wing on each side
14
15
Struts
Assemble as sh
These three ta
cemented tog
18 Front Tail
Center on
Fo
7
16
Important
Make wing creases & folds after joining 10 & 11
20 Wheels
cut in to center
Overlap & cement
17 Fold over as shown
This piece cemented last
19
Rear tail
center or
of 1 & fo
meet 9
Insert toothpick & rotate to make a smooth hole
Slip two halves over a toothpick as a guide & cement edge all around
- remove toothpick
21 Shock Absorber
Fold as shown
Insert landing gear axle 22 & do not cement
23
20
Wheels go on last after 21 is on plane and cement is dry
Tabs inserted in each end of 21 & cemented
Point axles outward & cement to 21
23 Hub
cement on end of axle
24 Tail S
insert with ce
on tip to con
top of 1
It shoulc
toward t

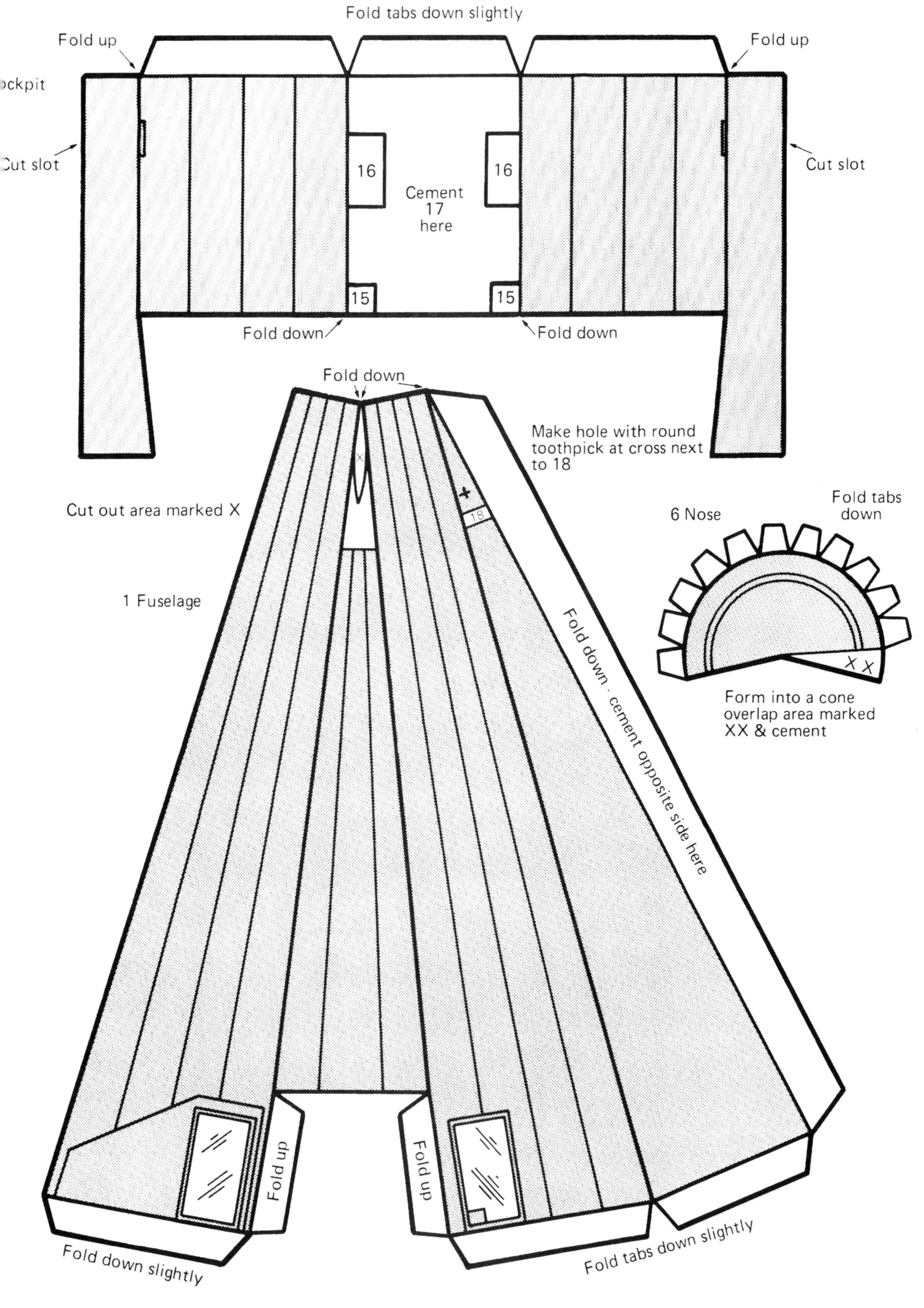

Fold tabs down slightly
Fold up
Fold up
ckpit
Cut slot
Cut slot
16
16
Cement
17
here
15
15
Fold down
Fold down
Fold down
Make hole with round toothpick at cross next to 18
18
Cut out area marked X
X
1 Fuselage
Fold down - cement opposite side here
6 Nose
Fold tabs down
XX
Form into a cone overlap area marked XX & cement
Fold up
Fold up
Fold down slightly
Fold tabs down slightly

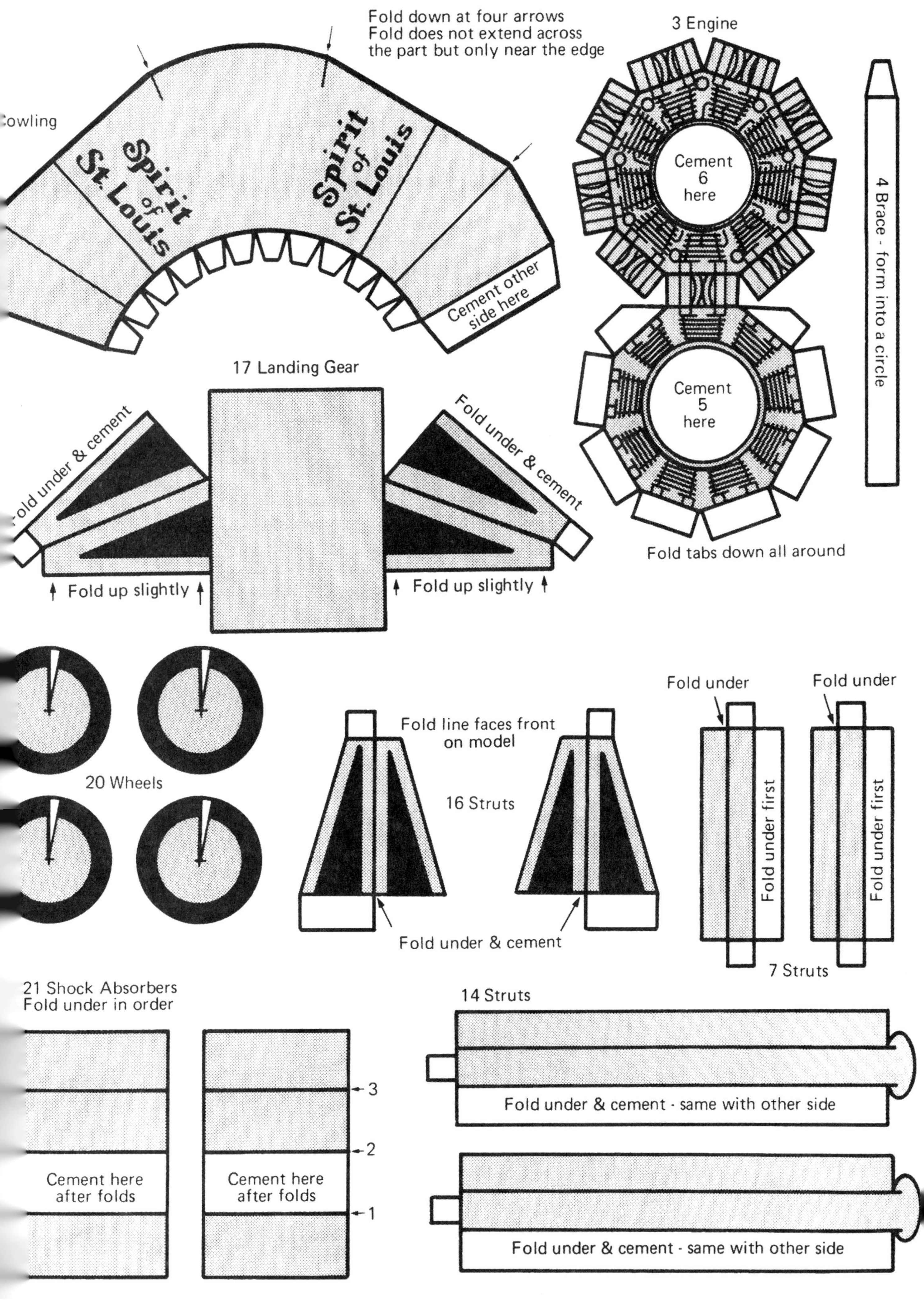
Fold down at four arrows
Fold does not extend across
the part but only near the edge
Cowling
Spirit of St. Louis
Spirit of St. Louis
Cement other side here
3 Engine
Cement 6 here
Cement 5 here
Fold tabs down all around
4 Brace - form into a circle
17 Landing Gear
Fold under & cement
Fold under & cement
Fold up slightly
Fold up slightly
20 Wheels
Fold line faces front on model
16 Struts
Fold under & cement
Fold under
Fold under
Fold under first
Fold under first
7 Struts
21 Shock Absorbers
Fold under in order
Cement here after folds
Cement here after folds
3
2
1
14 Struts
Fold under & cement - same with other side
Fold under & cement - same with other side

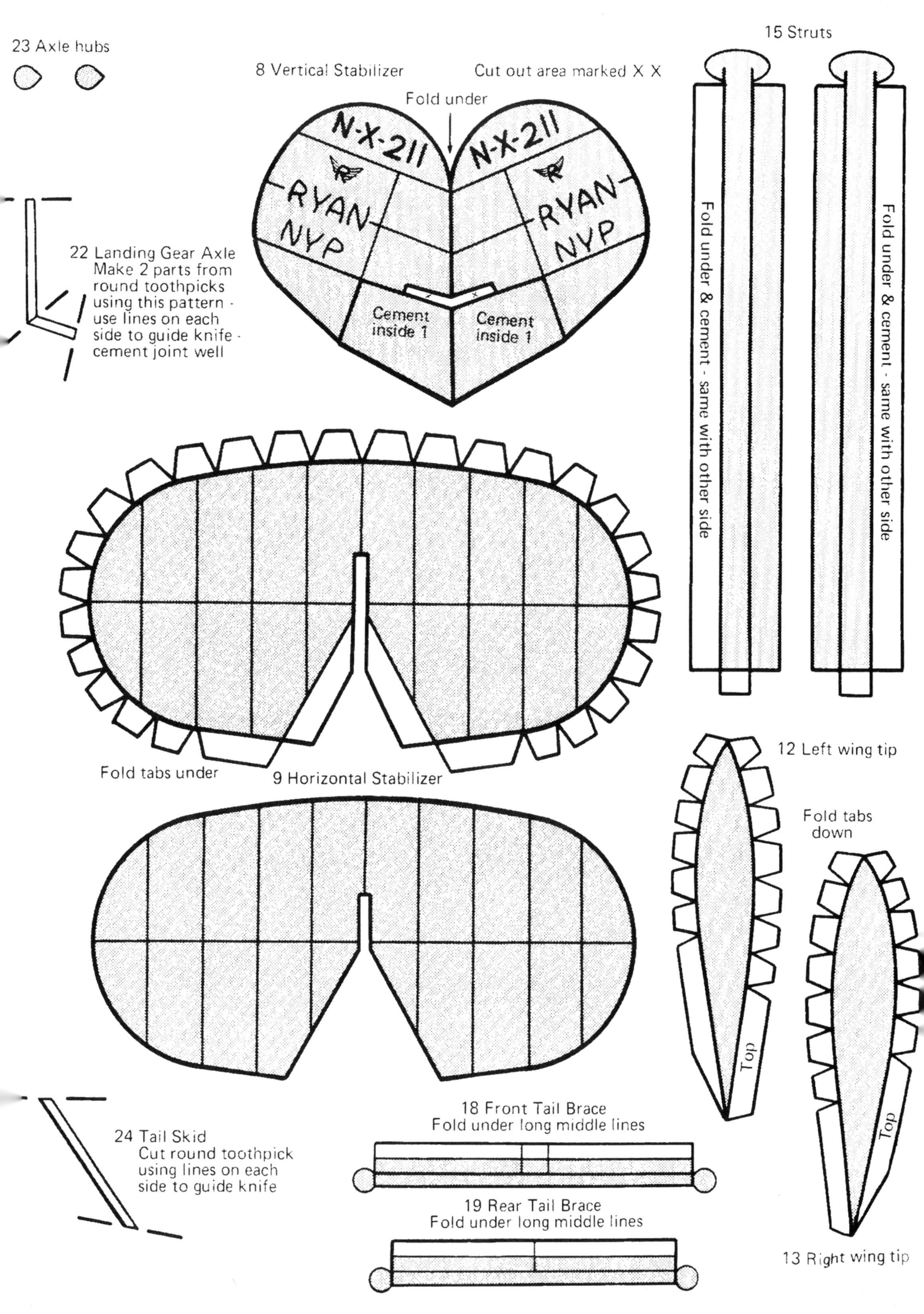
23 Axle hubs
8 Vertical Stabilizer
Cut out area marked X X
Fold under
N-X-211
RYAN
NYP
N-X-211
RYAN
NYP
Cement inside 1
Cement inside 1
15 Struts
Fold under & cement - same with other side
Fold under & cement - same with other side
22 Landing Gear Axle
Make 2 parts from round toothpicks using this pattern - use lines on each side to guide knife - cement joint well
Fold tabs under
9 Horizontal Stabilizer
12 Left wing tip
Fold tabs down
Top
Top
13 Right wing tip
24 Tail Skid
Cut round toothpick using lines on each side to guide knife
18 Front Tail Brace
Fold under long middle lines
19 Rear Tail Brace
Fold under long middle lines

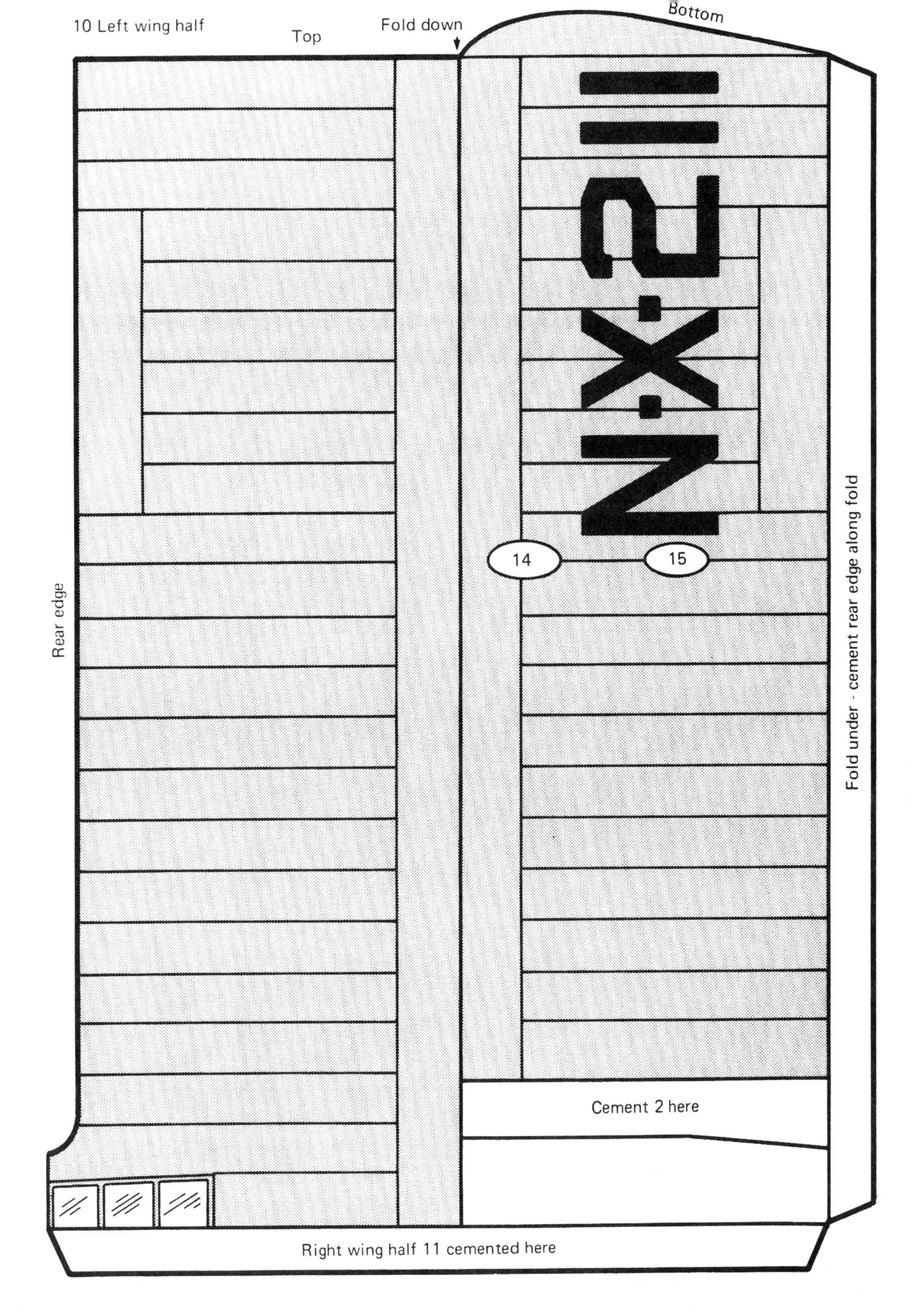
10 Left wing half
Top
Fold down
Bottom
N·X·211
14
15
Rear edge
Fold under - cement rear edge along fold
Cement 2 here
Right wing half 11 cemented here

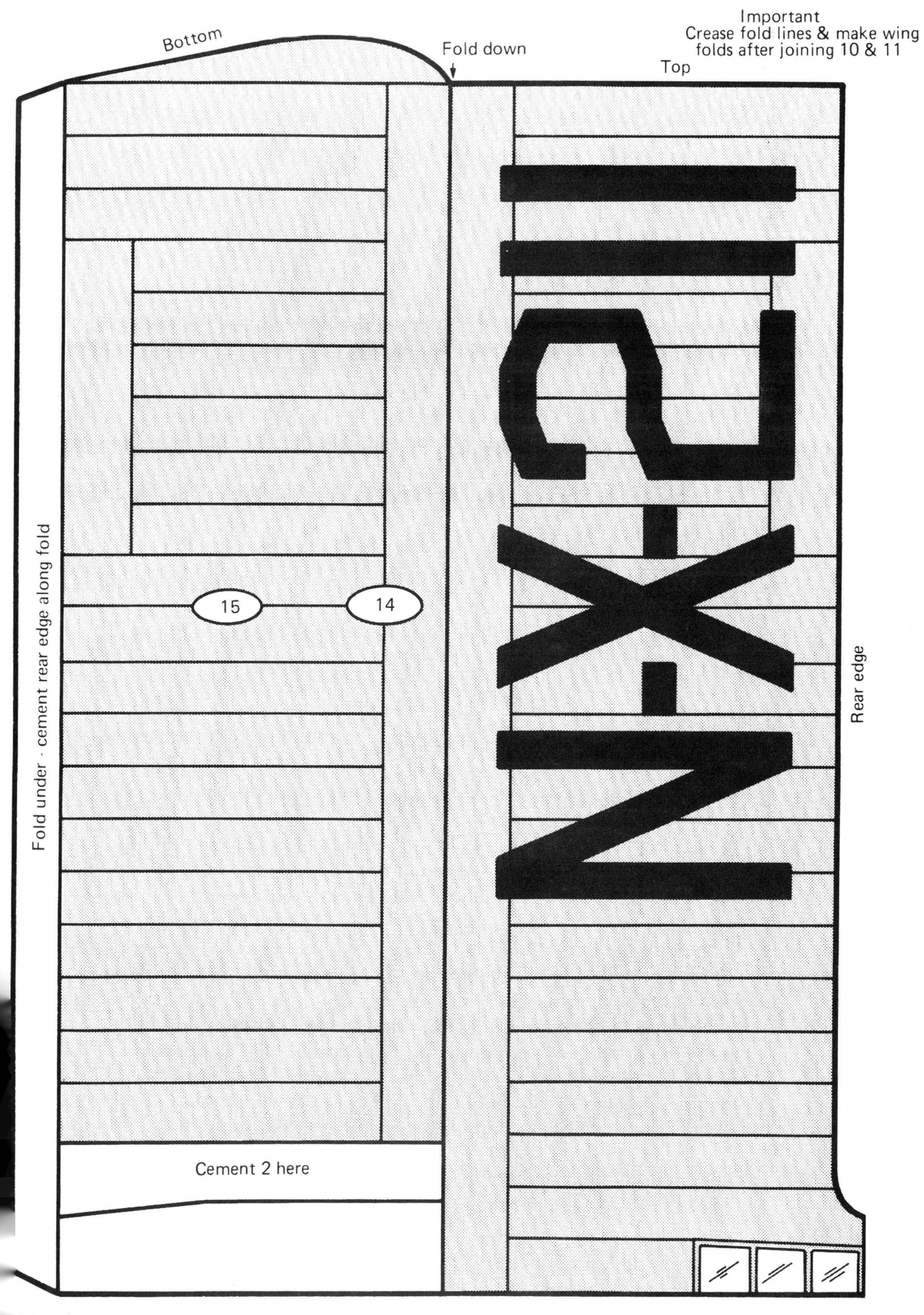
Important
Crease fold lines & make wing folds after joining 10 & 11
Bottom
Fold down
Top
N-X-15
15
14
Fold under - cement rear edge along fold
Rear edge
Cement 2 here
ight wing half

THE LOCKHEED *VEGA*

The Lockheed Vega was introduced in the late 1920s and was considered to be one of the most beautiful aircraft of its time. Built of laminated plywood, it was internally braced so there were no struts or wires, a very advanced design. The 1931 version was powered by an air-cooled Pratt and Whitney Wasp engine with over 400 horsepower. It could cruise at 150 mph and reach a top speed of 190 mph, a figure exceeded only by a few racing planes. It is best remembered as the plane flown by two famous American aviators of the 1930s, Amelia Earhart and Wiley Post. Amelia, in her red Vega, became the first woman to fly across the Atlantic. Post's all-white Vega was named the *Winnie Mae* after the daughter of its owner, F. C. Hall, an oilman who employed Post as his personal pilot. Hall was a flying buff and encouraged Post to use the plane to pursue racing and endurance records whenever he didn't need it. In 1931, assisted by navigator Harold Gatty, Post flew the *Winnie Mae* around the world in 8 days 15 hours and 51 minutes. The previous record had been held by Germany's *Graf Zeppelin,* an enormous 790-foot-long airship that had made the trip in 21 days in 1929.

Two developments after 1931 set the stage for Post's next flying record. One was the autopilot, a series of devices that could maintain an airplane on a straight and

AMELIA EARHART & WILEY POST WITH A *VEGA* ENGINE

level flight path without the aid of the pilot, and the other was the radio direction finder, which could home in on commercial radio stations as a navigational reference. The former would allow the pilot to get needed rest from constant attention to the controls and the latter would avoid errors in navigation due to relying solely on compass readings. Both innovations were installed on the *Winnie Mae,* and on July 22, 1933, Post completed his second around-the-world flight, alone, in 7 days 18 hours and 49½ minutes. The era when a plane's flight would be guided only by the steady hand and keen eyes of the pilot had come to a close.

Post went on to pioneer the idea of high-altitude flying. In the process, he discovered the Jet Stream and invented the pressurized flying suit, designing the first one himself. In later years improved versions would become standard equipment for jet pilots and astronauts alike. A native of Oklahoma, he had lost an eye in an accident while working in the oil fields, but labored through long hours of practice to compensate for his handicap and become a first-rate pilot. Post and famed humorist Will Rogers were lost in a crash near Point Barrow, Alaska while Post was flying Rogers to gather material for his syndicated column.

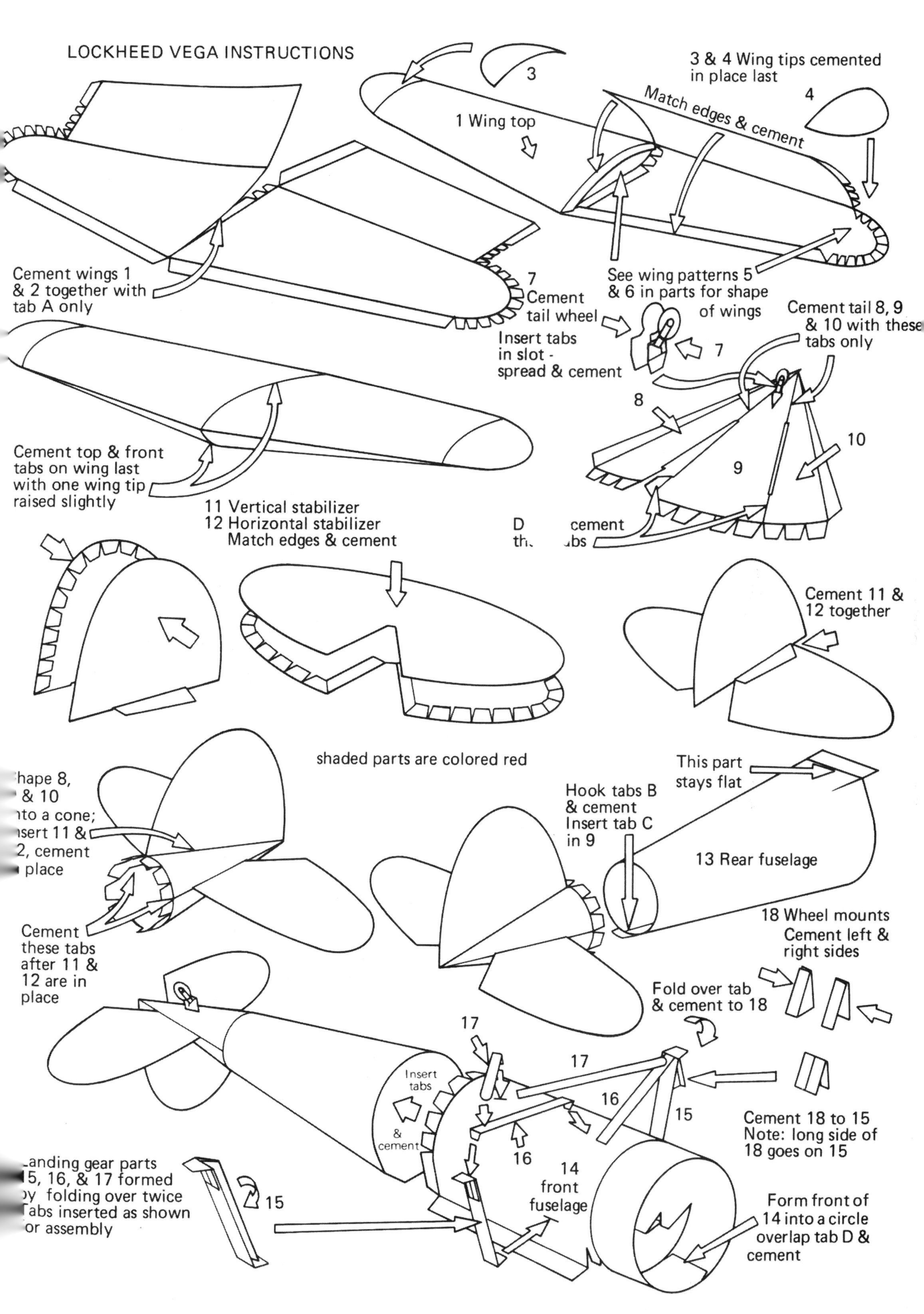
LOCKHEED VEGA INSTRUCTIONS
3
3 & 4 Wing tips cemented in place last
4
Match edges & cement
1 Wing top
Cement wings 1 & 2 together with tab A only
7
Cement tail wheel
See wing patterns 5 & 6 in parts for shape of wings
Insert tabs in slot - spread & cement
7
Cement tail 8, 9 & 10 with these tabs only
8
10
9
Cement top & front tabs on wing last with one wing tip raised slightly
11 Vertical stabilizer
12 Horizontal stabilizer
Match edges & cement
cement
Cement 11 & 12 together
shaded parts are colored red
This part stays flat
Hook tabs B & cement
Insert tab C in 9
13 Rear fuselage
Cement these tabs after 11 & 12 are in place
18 Wheel mounts
Cement left & right sides
Fold over tab & cement to 18
17
17
Insert tabs
& cement
16
15
16
14 front fuselage
Cement 18 to 15
Note: long side of 18 goes on 15
15
Form front of 14 into a circle overlap tab D & cement

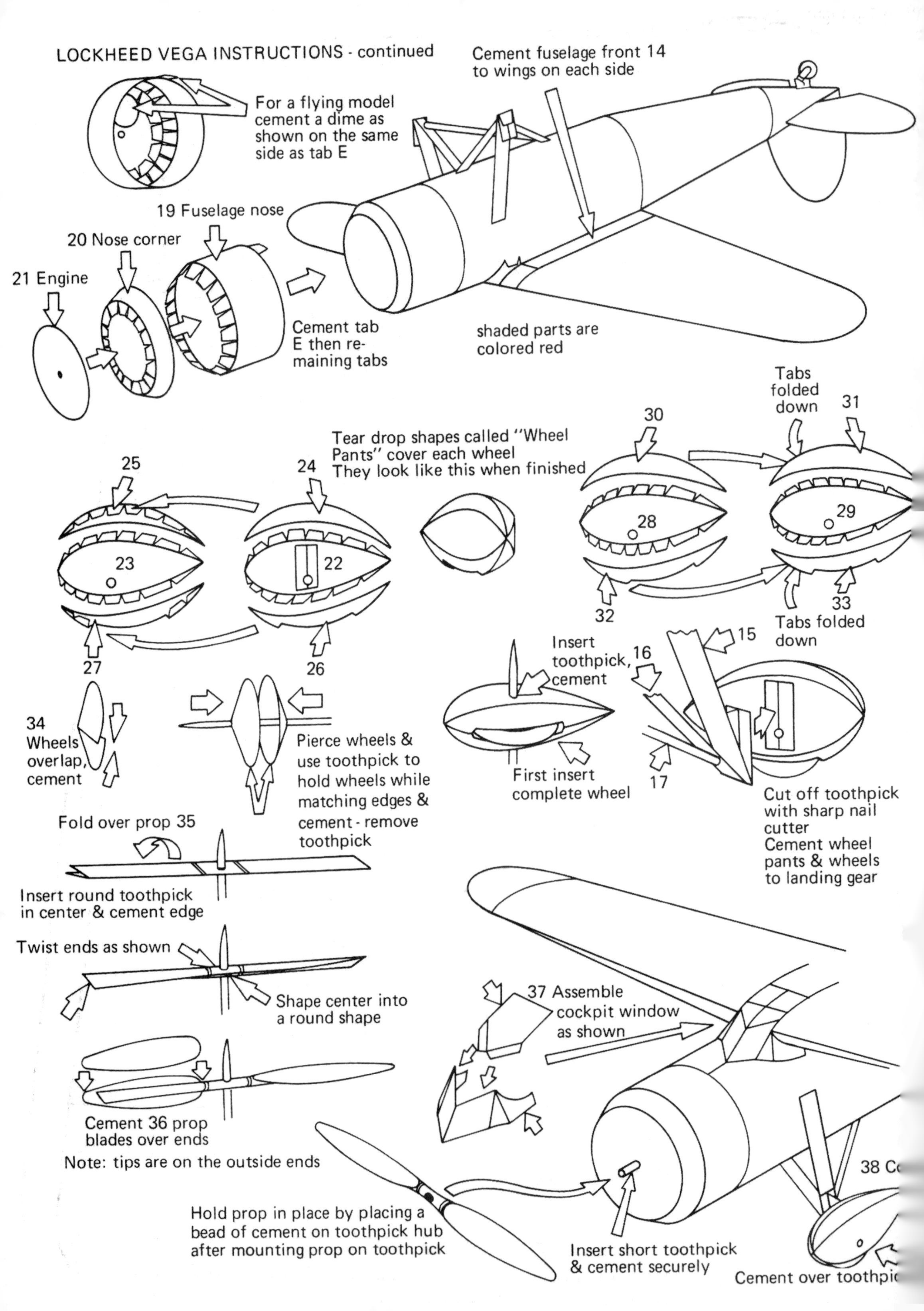

LOCKHEED VEGA INSTRUCTIONS - continued
Cement fuselage front 14 to wings on each side
For a flying model cement a dime as shown on the same side as tab E
19 Fuselage nose
20 Nose corner
21 Engine
Cement tab E then remaining tabs
shaded parts are colored red
Tabs folded down
30
31
Tear drop shapes called "Wheel Pants" cover each wheel They look like this when finished
25
24
23
22
28
29
32
33
Tabs folded down
27
26
Insert toothpick, cement
16
15
34 Wheels overlap, cement
Pierce wheels & use toothpick to hold wheels while matching edges & cement - remove toothpick
First insert complete wheel
17
Cut off toothpick with sharp nail cutter
Cement wheel pants & wheels to landing gear
Fold over prop 35
Insert round toothpick in center & cement edge
Twist ends as shown
Shape center into a round shape
37 Assemble cockpit window as shown
Cement 36 prop blades over ends
Note: tips are on the outside ends
38 C
Hold prop in place by placing a bead of cement on toothpick hub after mounting prop on toothpick
Insert short toothpick & cement securely
Cement over toothpi

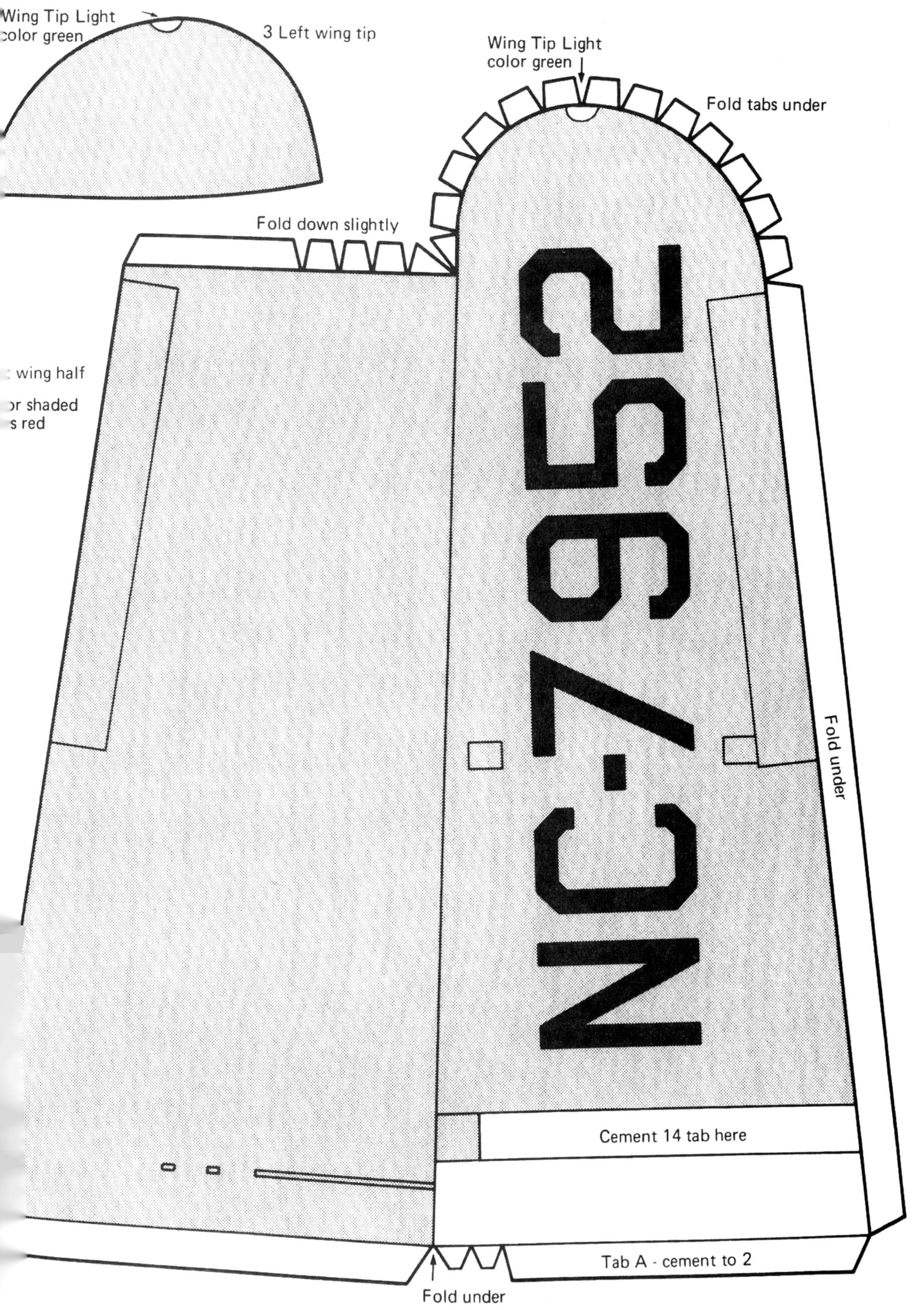
Wing Tip Light
color green
3 Left wing tip
Wing Tip Light
color green
Fold tabs under
Fold down slightly
Fold under
Cement 14 tab here
Tab A - cement to 2
Fold under

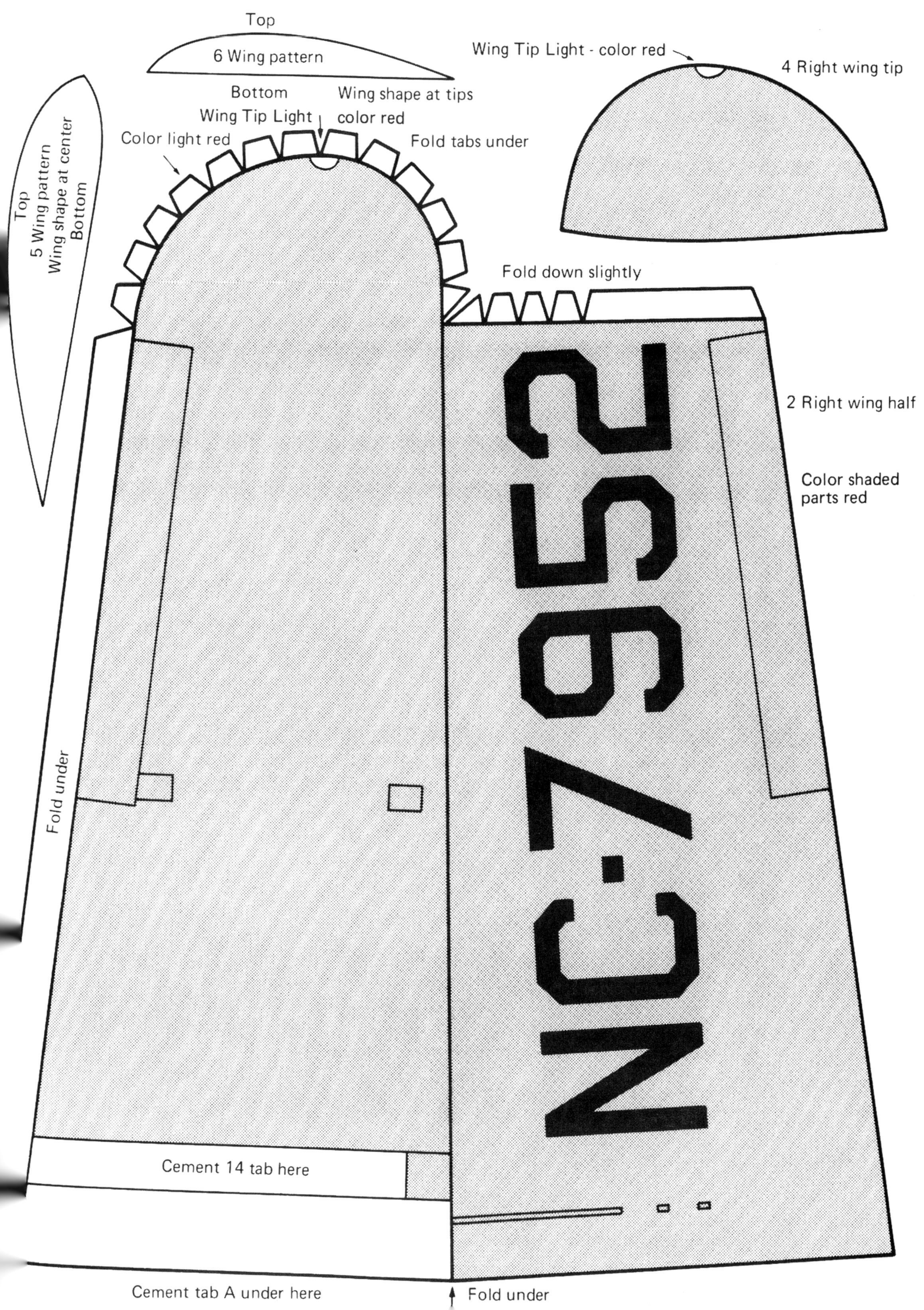
Top
6 Wing pattern
Bottom
Wing shape at tips
color red
Wing Tip Light
Color light red
Fold tabs under
Top
5 Wing pattern
Wing shape at center
Bottom
Wing Tip Light - color red
4 Right wing tip
Fold down slightly
NC-7952
2 Right wing half
Color shaded parts red
Fold under
Cement 14 tab here
Cement tab A under here
Fold under

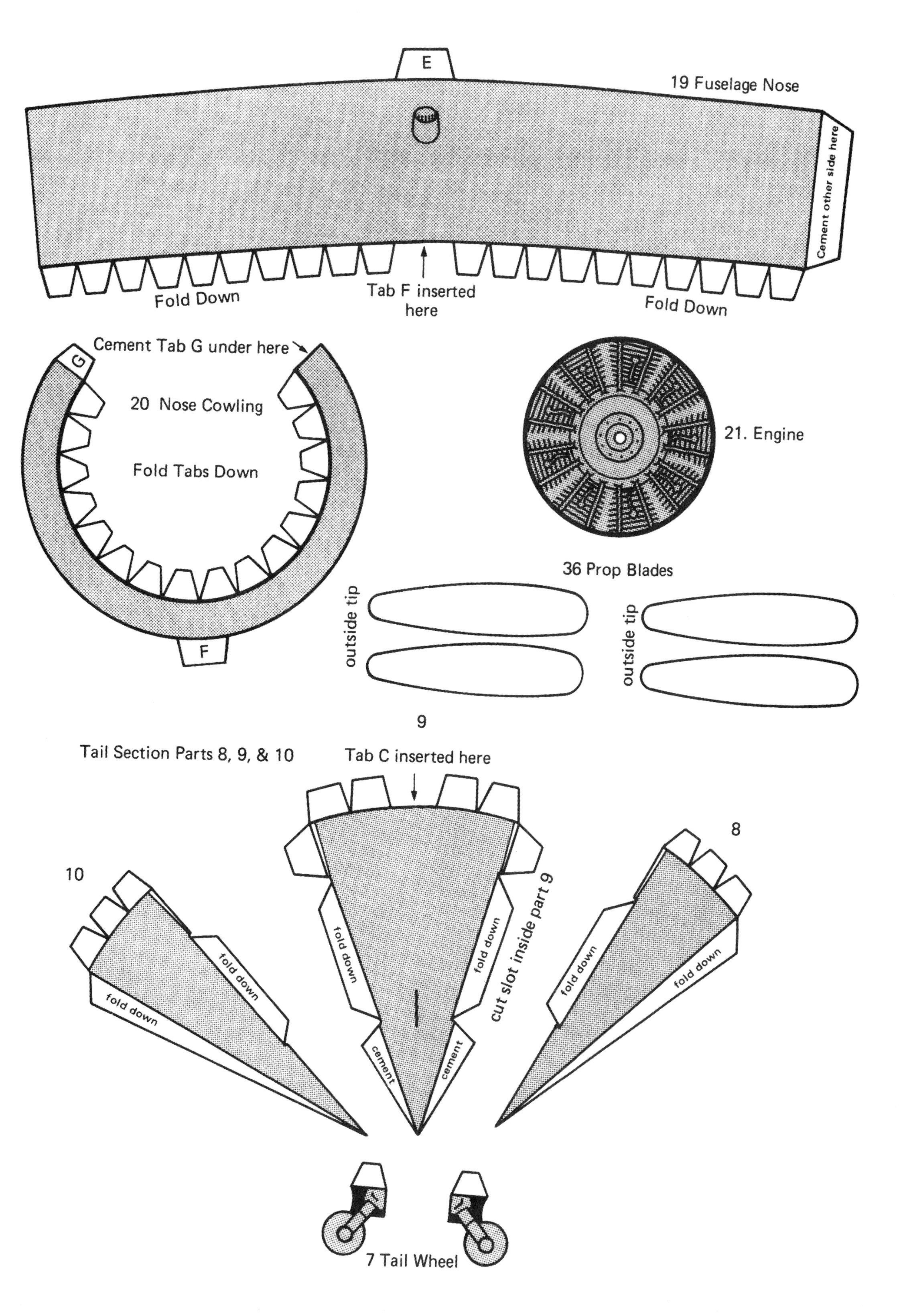
E
19 Fuselage Nose
Cement other side here
Fold Down
Tab F inserted here
Fold Down
Cement Tab G under here
G
20 Nose Cowling
Fold Tabs Down
F
21. Engine
36 Prop Blades
outside tip
outside tip
9
Tail Section Parts 8, 9, & 10
Tab C inserted here
8
10
cut slot inside part 9
fold down
fold down
fold down
fold down
fold down
fold down
cement
cement
7 Tail Wheel

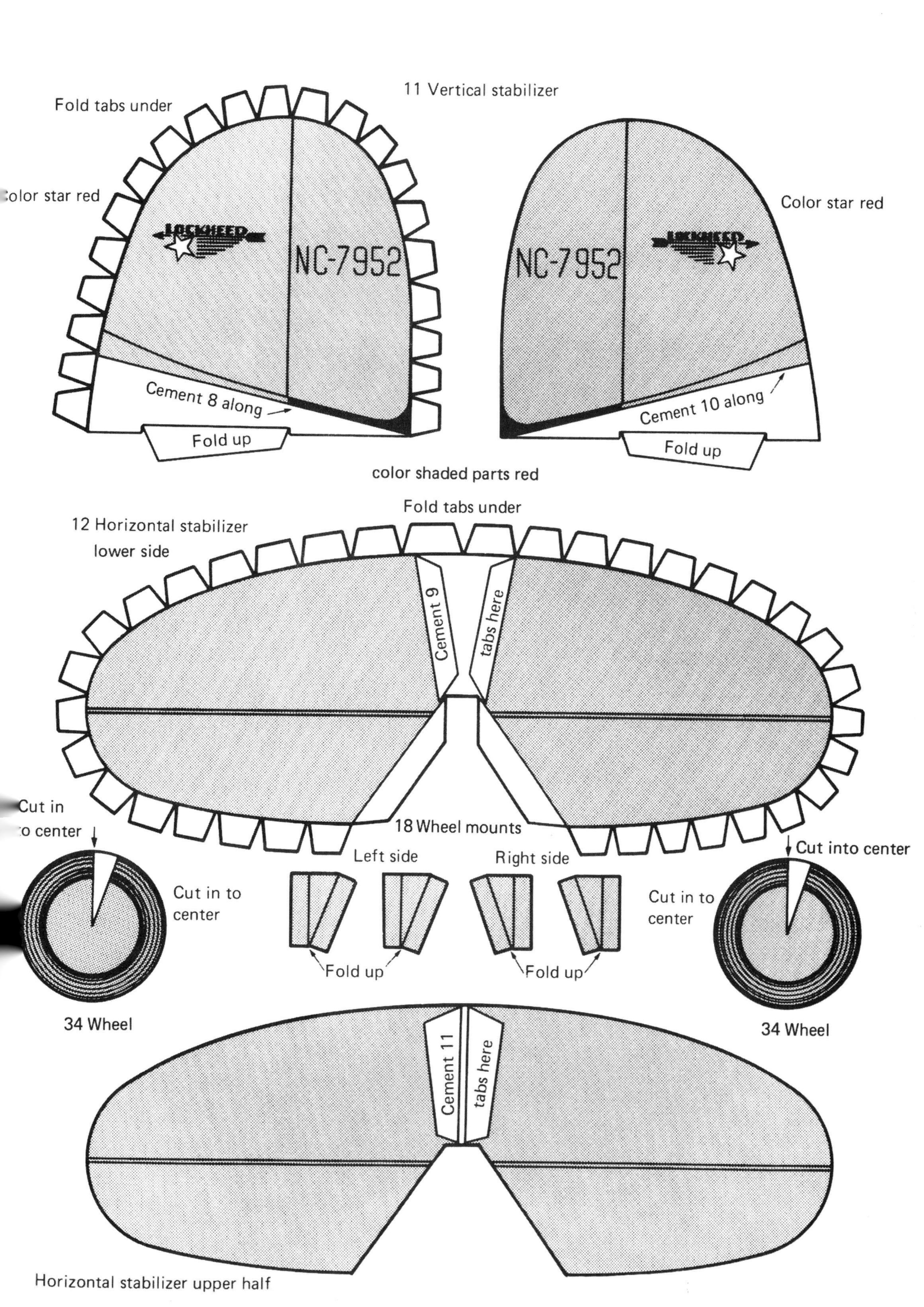

11 Vertical stabilizer
Fold tabs under
Color star red
LOCKHEED
NC-7952
Color star red
LOCKHEED
NC-7952
Cement 8 along
Cement 10 along
Fold up
Fold up
color shaded parts red
Fold tabs under
12 Horizontal stabilizer
lower side
Cement 9
tabs here
Cut in
to center
18 Wheel mounts
Left side
Right side
Cut into center
Cut in to
center
Cut in to
center
Fold up
Fold up
34 Wheel
34 Wheel
Cement 11
tabs here
Horizontal stabilizer upper half

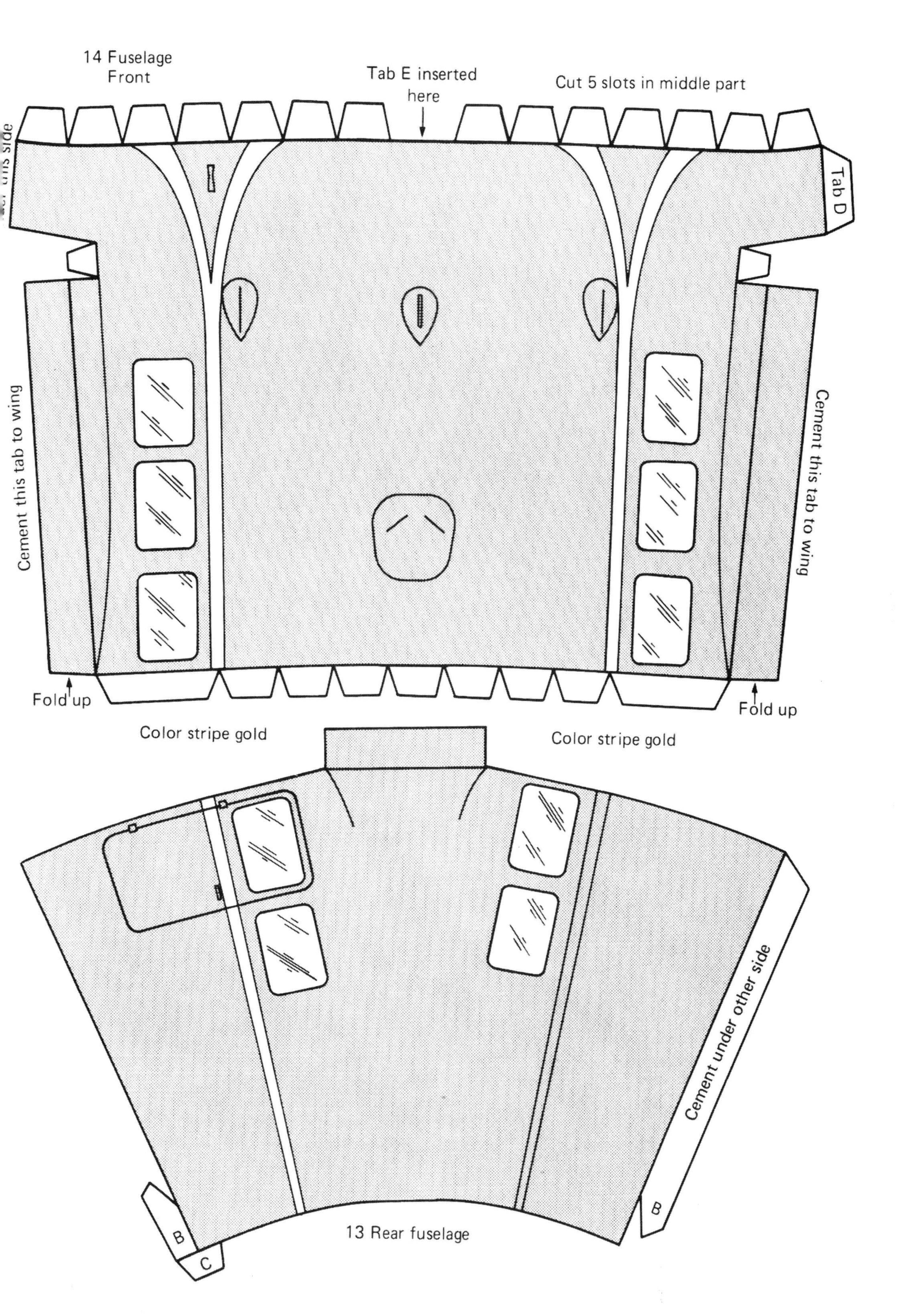

14 Fuselage
Front
Tab E inserted
here
Cut 5 slots in middle part
Tab D
Cement this tab to wing
Cement this tab to wing
Fold up
Fold up
Color stripe gold
Color stripe gold
Cement under other side
B
B
C
13 Rear fuselage

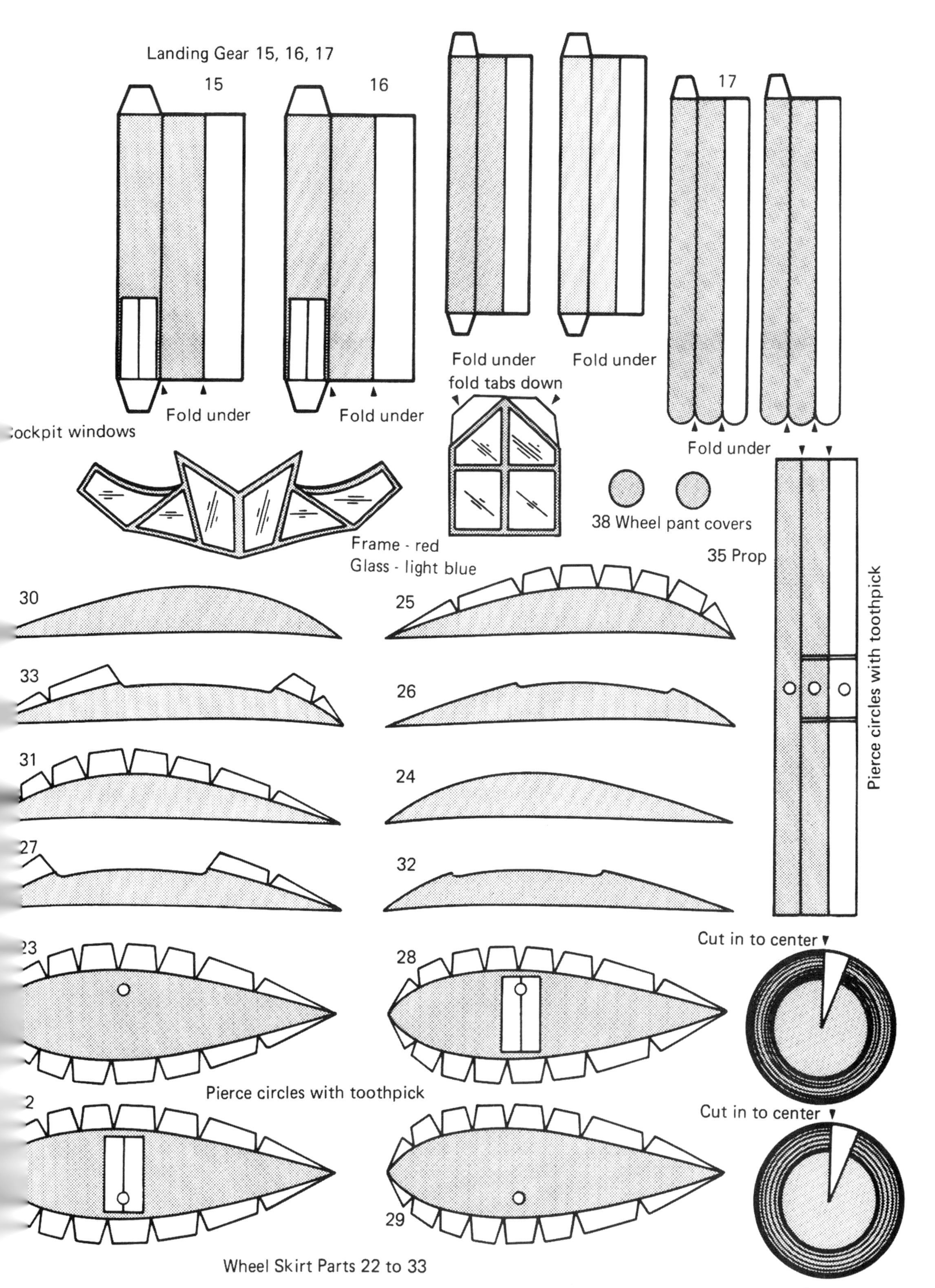
Landing Gear 15, 16, 17
15
16
17
Fold under
Fold under
Fold under
fold tabs down
Fold under
Fold under
Cockpit windows
38 Wheel pant covers
Frame - red
Glass - light blue
35 Prop
Pierce circles with toothpick
30
25
33
26
31
24
27
32
23
28
Cut in to center
Pierce circles with toothpick
22
Cut in to center
29
Wheel Skirt Parts 22 to 33
34 Wheels

The Bell XS - 1

With World War II and the development of the jet engine, flying speeds close to the speed of sound became a reality. The only forseeable obstacle to propelling planes faster and faster lay in a strange effect that was encountered when approaching the speed of sound: severe buffeting and loss of control capable of damaging or destroying the aircraft. It was dubbed "the sound barrier" appropriately enough and became the subject of intense study by the leading aircraft designers. The U.S. government funded Bell Aircraft to build a special research aircraft specifically for the purpose of learning more about very high-speed, high-altitude flight. The result was the Bell XS-1, a rocket-powered craft launched from the bomb bay of a B-29 bomber and flown in the late 1940s. On October 17, 1947, Charles Yeager flew the XS-1 at 763 mph to become the first pilot to fly faster than the speed of sound without suffering serious ill effects. The "sound barrier" was broken. At the time the accomplishment was considered such a breakthrough that official confirmation was not released to the press until months later. The XS-1 would achieve a top speed of 967 mph and a maximum altitude of 70,140 feet before being replaced with the more advanced XI-A. In 1950 it was donated to the National Air Museum, Smithsonian Institution.

BELL XS-1 INSTRUCTIONS

Color - orange on all shaded areas
Insignia : white star on blue background
white bars on each side of stars

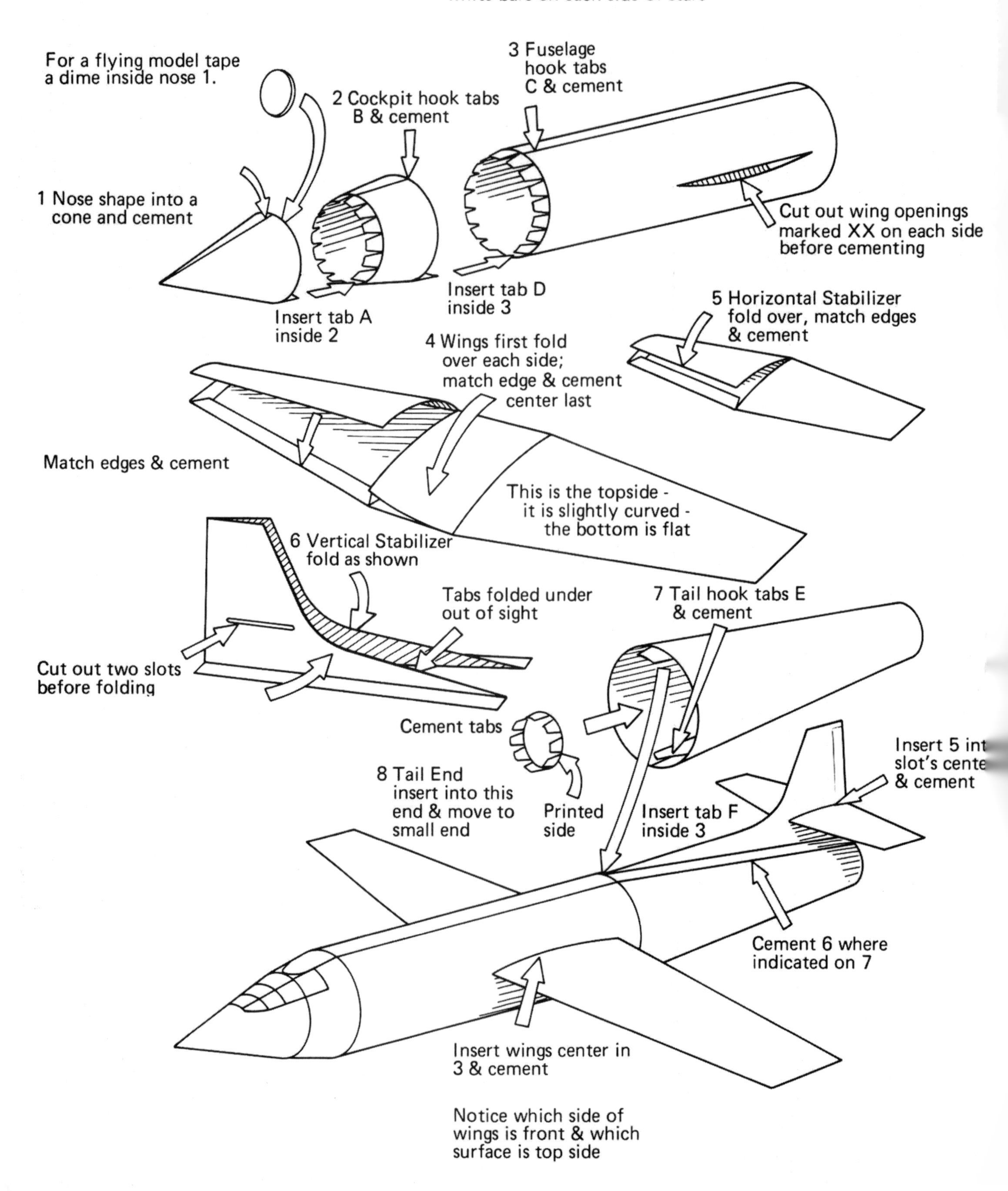

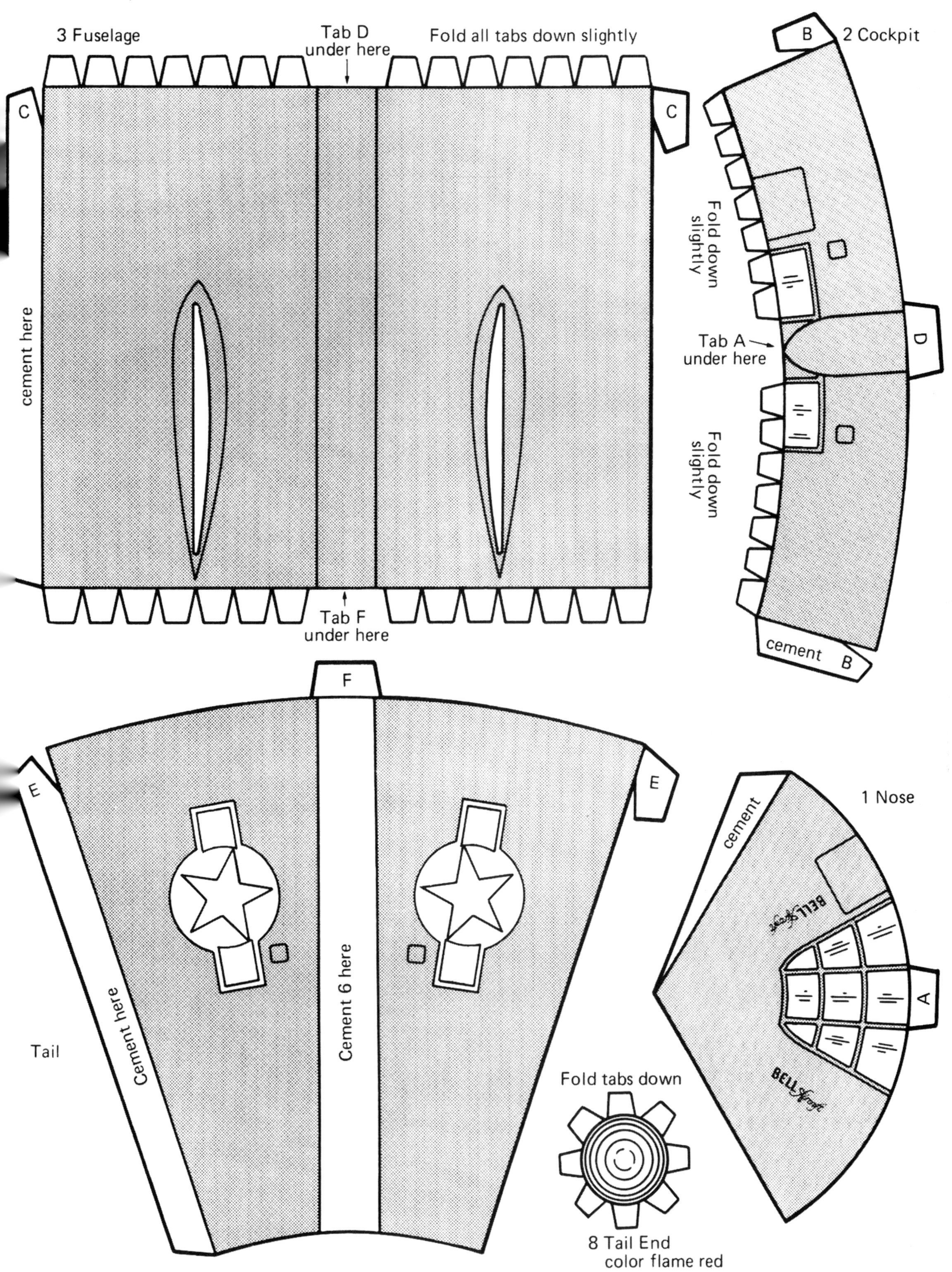
3 Fuselage
Tab D
under here
Fold all tabs down slightly
C
C
cement here
Tab F
under here
B
2 Cockpit
Fold down
slightly
Tab A
under here
D
Fold down
slightly
cement B
F
E
E
Cement here
Cement 6 here
Tail
1 Nose
cement
BELL Aircraft
A
BELL Aircraft
Fold tabs down
8 Tail End
color flame red

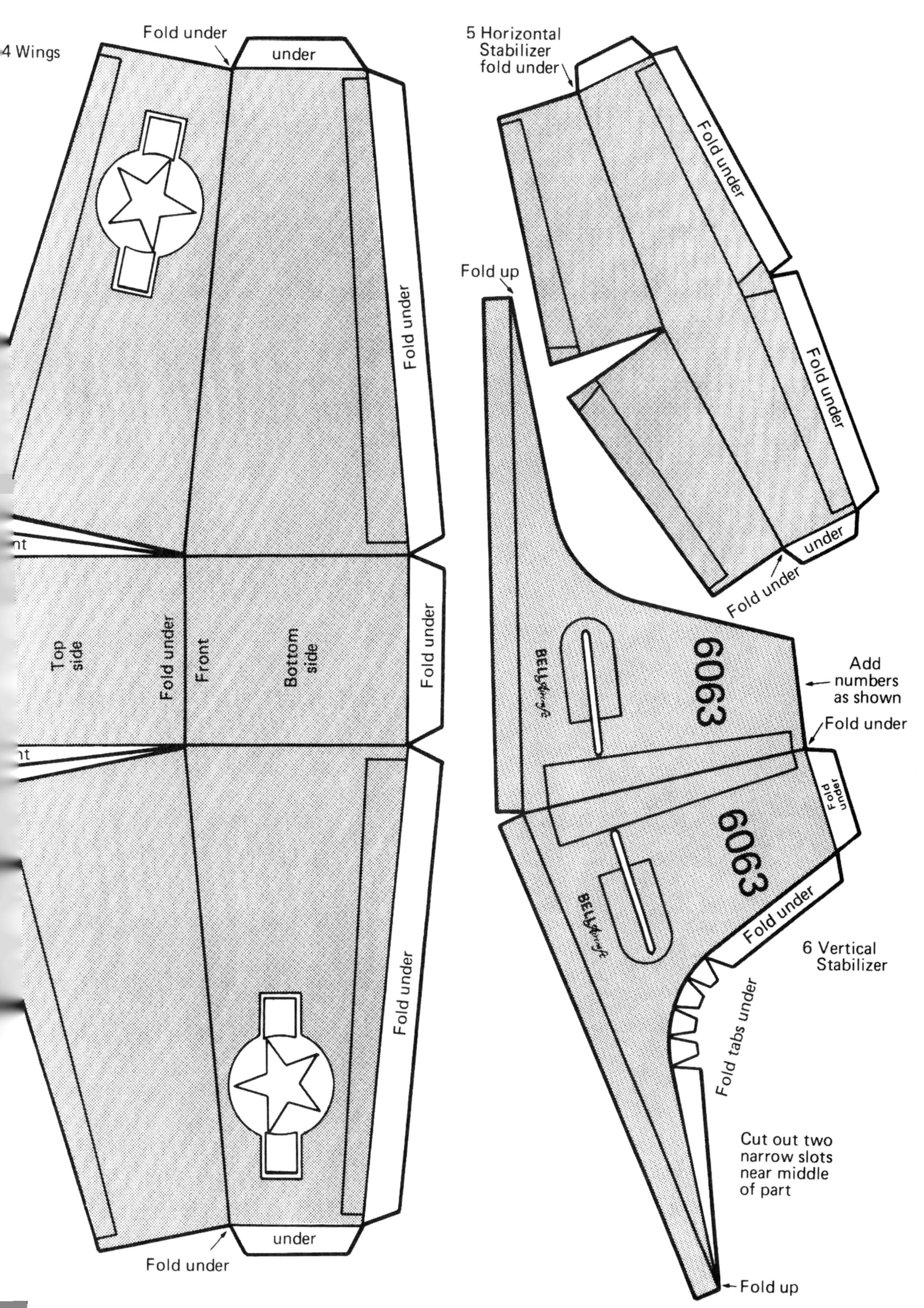

4 Wings
Fold under
under
Fold under
Top side
Fold under
Front
Bottom side
Fold under
Fold under
under
Fold under
5 Horizontal Stabilizer fold under
Fold under
Fold under
under
Fold under
Fold up
6063
Add numbers as shown
Fold under
Fold under
6063
Fold under
6 Vertical Stabilizer
Fold tabs under
Cut out two narrow slots near middle of part
Fold up